# Words Of The King

## The Illustrated Wisdom Of Cormac Mac Airt

Written and Illustrated by Olivia Wylie

Copyright © 2022, Leafing Out Books
Written and Illustrated by Olivia Wylie
ISBN 978-17-343-27-168

All rights reserved. No part of this publication may be reproduced, distributed, or transmitted in any form or by any means, including photocopying, recording, or other electronic or mechanical methods, without the prior written permission of the publisher, except in the case of brief quotations embodied in critical reviews and certain other noncommercial uses permitted by copyright law.
For permission requests, write to the publisher, addressed "Attention: Illustrator" at olivia@leafingoutgardening.com

# Introduction

*"In his reign the rivers of Ireland were overflowing with fish, the forests groaned under their load of fruit, and the beehives dripped with honey. Peace reigned, crops grew in abundance and cows gave generously of their milk."*

These are how the years are remembered, in The Annals of Clonmacnoise, when Cormac Mac Aírt sat the throne at Tara. The hundred-and-sixteenth Ard Rí is the man who we think of when we imagine the High Kings: just, wise, calm. Good company at the feast, terrible enemy in battle. And always, always, caring for his people.
But who was Cormac Mac Aírt?
It's difficult to be completely sure, so many years since he ruled. He had many names:
Cormac mac Aírt—son of Art—Cormac ua Cuinnthe—Grandson of Conn—Voice of Cashel, Lawgiver, Ulfada—Longbeard—and of course, Ard Rí. In later times, he was sometimes called the Irish Solomon. Sources generally agree on a few facts: he was the son of Art the Melancholy and grandson of Conn of the Hundred Battles. It's generally agreed that he was born circa 190 A.D. near Tara. His rule encompassed forty years, and he died in 266 A.D. to be buried at Ros-na-Riogh. Beyond that, we have to pick our way carefully through lovely thickets of legend, following glimmers of truth.

Cormac Mac Airt has a hundred and one stories told in his name. They say he was suckled by a wolf as a babe. They say he stopped a castle from falling into the sea by telling a truth. They say he loved a lady of the Sidhe, and enraged a druid. His story has been stitched over by the tongues of a thousand storytellers. Even Robert Howard of Conan the Barbarian fame borrowed the name of Cormac Mac Art for some rather—shall we say energetic?— tale-spinning. As one classic text put it rather wryly, 'his reign furnished, indeed, many rich themes for the romantic poets and story-tellers of subsequent ages'

**B**ut what is held up again and again is the King's wisdom. The recorded annals tell us that Cormac founded three schools at Tara: one for teaching the art of war, the second for the study of history, and the third for the study of law and its proper use. But stories tell us more than that. The Reverend John Healy records this in his work, 'Insula Sanctorum et Doctorum',

> "The Feis of Tara, then, was in existence before the time of Cormac; but it was seldom convened, and had almost fallen into disuse. Cormac it was, who made arrangements for the regular meetings of that great parliament of the nation, and provided adequate accommodation for the assembled notables. Here we are on firm historic ground and can enter into more minute details with security.
> The object of this Feis of Tara was mainly three-fold. First, to enact and promulgate what was afterwards called the *cain*-law, which was obligatory in all the territories and tribes of the kingdom, as distinguished from the *urradhus*, or local law. Secondly, to test and sanction the Annals of Erin. For this purpose each of the local Seanachies or historians brought in a record of the notable events that took place in his own territory. These were publicly read for the assembly, and when duly authenticated were entered on the great record of the King of Tara, called afterwards the "Saltair of Tara." Thirdly, to register in the same great national record the genealogies of the ruling families, to assess the taxes, and settle all cases of disputed succession among the tribes of the kingdom. Too often this was done by the strong hand; but it was Cormac's idea to fix the succession, as far as possible, according to definite principles amongst the ruling families. The absence of a strong central government to enforce this most wise provision was one main cause of the subsequent distracted state of the kingdom.
> This great national assembly, convened for these purposes, met once every three years. The session continued for a week, beginning the third day before, and ending the third day after November day. When so many turbulent chieftains, oftentimes at feud amongst themselves, met together, it was necessary to keep the peace of Tara by very stringent regulations, enforced under the most rigorous penalties. It is to Cormac's prudent forethought we owe these regulations, which were afterwards inviolably observed as the law of Tara. Every provincial king and every sub-king had his own fixed place allotted to him near the High King by the marshals of Tara; and every chief was bound to take his seat under the place where his shield was hung upon the wall. Brawling was strictly forbidden, and to wound another was a capital crime."

**I**t's said that Cormac convened another great gathering as well: a conclave of the fillid and brehon of those days, all together at Tara, to ensure that the laws and the tales were agreed upon and known by all. It was at these gatherings that the Brehon Laws were codified.

**T**he tales of Cormac Mac Airt's life are so wild that we have to ask: was there a real man named Cormac Mac Airt? Or was he a figure like King Arthur, the dream of a good king told by people longing for just and benevolent rule? He is recorded in The Annals of Clonmacnoise, true. And his tales are recorded in the Book of Leinster, the Yellow Book of Lecan and the Book of Ballymote. But these were all written centuries after he ruled. His story is set solidly in the Heroic Age of Ireland, where the facts are less sure than the feelings of the time. There are no stones that bear his name or his likeness.

**B**ut there are signs that he was once a man. If you stand on Tara, you'll see that the outlines of Cormac's house are still there within the circle of Rath na Riogh. The stream flowing from the well on which he built the first mill in Ireland still flows down the eastern slope of Tara Hill. Even the well on the western slope where Cormac's kitchen was built has been discovered. The north-western seating area where he corrected the false judgment of King Mac Con about the trespass of a widow's sheep may still be traced. And there is a book of wisdom: the Tecosca Cormaic, known in English as the Counsels of Cormac or the The instructions of King Cormac Mac Airt.

**A**ttributed to Cormac and his son Cairbre, The Tecosca Cormaic is part of the Irish gnomic text tradition. It was written in the form of a dialogue containing a list of qualities. Analogous lists appear in contemporary sources such as Togail Bruidne Da Derga, Fled Bricrenn and Genemain Áeda Slane, showing that these lists were common to early Irish wisdom and legal literature, an integral part of the Old Irish narrative style. Following this traditional format, the Counsels use a question-answer technique: a question asked by Cairbre introduces the topic, and Cormac answers, often finishing his remarks by turning the originating question into a statement. A number of examples showing this pattern exist throughout the text:

### Counsel Three

Cid as dech do less túathe? … dech do less túathe in sin,
'What is best for the good of a tribe? … that is best for the good of a tribe'.

### Counsel Four

Cadeat ada flatha 7 cuirmthige? … it é sin adae flatha 7 cormthige,
'What are the dues of a chief and of an ale-house? … those are the dues of a chief and of an ale-house'.

*Note: when a word is unreadable in the original manuscript, it is replaced by a number.

### Counsel Five

Cid asa ngaibther flaithemnas for túathaib 7 chlandaib 7 chenélaib? … A feib chrotha… gaibther.

'Whence is chieftaincy taken over kingdoms, and clans, and kins? … By virtue of shape …it is taken'.

### Counsel Six

Caté téchta flatha? … ar is triasna téchta sin miditir ríg 7 flaithi.

'What is proper of a ruler? … for it is by those qualities kings and rulers are
Judged'.

### Counsel Seven

Cia bátar do bésa intan ropsa gilla? …ar is triasna bésu sin roscgat óic
corbat sen 7 ríaglaích.
'What were your habits when you were a lad? … For it is through those habits that the young become old and kingly warriors'.

### Counsel Eight

Cia bátar do gníma intan ropsa gilla? …rop íat sin mo gníma.
'What were your deeds when you were a lad? … those were my deeds'.

It cannot be known whether we have the majority of the Tecosca, or only a fraction. New fragments are regularly discovered by scholars, often mixed into other works. The entries of the Tecosca that have survived as a coherent text come to us from the Book of Lecan, the Book of Ballymote, and the Book of Leinster.

The entire manuscript was first well-recorded in 1745 by Tadhg Ua Neachtain, under the title 'Teagasg Riogh'. It was edited and re-translated in 1909 by Kuno Meyer as 'The instructions of King Cormac Mac Airt: Tecosca Cormaic' in the Todd lecture series, Volume 15. Finally, it was reworked and revised by Thomas Cleary as 'The Counsels of Cormac: An ancient Irish guide to leadership' in 2004. An electric edition was compiled by Beatrix Färber and funded by University College as part of CELT: Corpus of Electronic Texts: a project of University College, Cork, in 2017.

Going forward, I'll be drawing from these translations to create accessible, illustrated pages that will make these ancient words on what it is to be a good leader and a good people easier on the eyes and the minds of modern readers. In the original text, the paragraphs were organized first with good qualities, and then with warnings and evil qualities. I have re-organized these passages so that good and bad as the Old Irish understood it are seen together, each a mirror of the entry before it. In the appendix, thoughts on each illustration are labeled with their original place in the Tecosca and a few reflections on their cultural significance.

True words should not be trapped in dusty tomes and read by scholars alone. They should dance across the pages in our hands and the thoughts in our minds.
May what follows help the words be true for you.

**Cormac, grandson of Conn,** said Cairbre, "What were your habits when you were a lad?"
"Not hard to tell," said Cormac

"I was a listener in the woods,
I was a gazer at the stars
I was blind to men's secrets

I was silent in the wild places
I was talkative in the gathering
I was genial in the mead-hall
I was harsh in battle

I was kind in friendship,
I was a physician of the sick
I was gentle towards the feeble
I was strong against the powerful

I was not harsh, lest I should be satirized
I did not cling, lest I should be burdensome
I was not chattering, though I was clever
I was not arrogant, though I was wise

I was not boastful, though I was strong
I was not venturesome, though I was swift
I did not deride the old, though I was young
I was not bragging, though I was capable

I would not speak about another in his absence
I would not reproach, but I would praise
I would not ask, but I would give

For it is through these habits
that the young
grow strong
and proud."

# Cormac, grandson of Conn, said Cairbre,

"what is best for the good of a tribe?"
"Not hard to tell," said Cormac.

"A gathering of good folk,
often taking counsel,
An inquiring mind,

Consulting the wise,
Quelling every evil,
Ensuring every good

Often holding court,
Following tradition,
Upholding law

A chieftain who leads justly,
A law that is administered fairly,
staving off the crushing of
the weak

Friendship without fickleness,
Strength without vainglory,
Showing integrity
to foe and kin alike

Generous pledges,
complete repayment,
just rulings,

Honest witnesses,
Bargains kept honestly,
Interest on loss,

Fair weights and fair measures,
Ready hiring for the season's work,
Promises offered in accordance with your station,

Lending without stint,
Loans for wholesome purposes,
An equivalent for every good;
A dignified response, legitimate measure

Studying every art,
Knowledge of every language,
Skill in many crafts,
Argumentation using legal precedents,
Passing judgment with wisdom

Giving alms to the poor,
giving justice, giving mercy,
Honest contracts

Attention to elders and dismissal to fools,
Never a forgetting of the needs of the folk
Never the chieftain at feast when the people hunger,
These things are best for the good of the tribe."

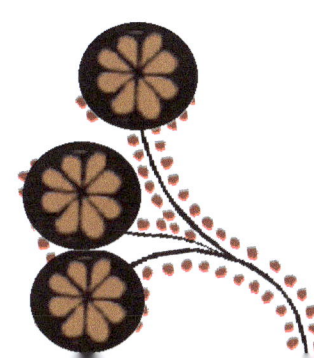

# Of the folk, Cormac said to Cairbre:

Everyone is wise
till he sells his inheritance,

everyone is foolish
till he buys land,

everyone is a friend
till it comes to debts,

everyone is respected
till he is satirized,

everyone is slothful
till it comes to marrying,

everyone is rowdy
till it comes to religion,

everyone is hospitable
till he turns one from the door,

everyone is a roving warrior
till he takes up farming,

everyone is a servant
till he builds a house,

everyone is sound of mind
till he drinks spirits

everyone is decorous
till he commits adultery,

everyone is tranquil
till he has children,

everyone is confident
till he begins to quarrel,

everyone is a citizen
till he is denounced,

everyone is cheerful
till he meets with bad luck,

everyone is bold
till he meets with a refusal.

everyone is a citizen
till he is denounced,

everyone is cheerful
till he meets with bad luck,

One who prospers has dignity
One who suffers illness has shame
A young person who keeps these things in mind
will be lovable in youth,
venerable in age,
true in word,
honorable in appearance.
If he is amiable, humble, obedient, earnest in word and deed, then he will be respected in spite of his station, he will be wise in spite of his years, and his future will be assured with God and folk.

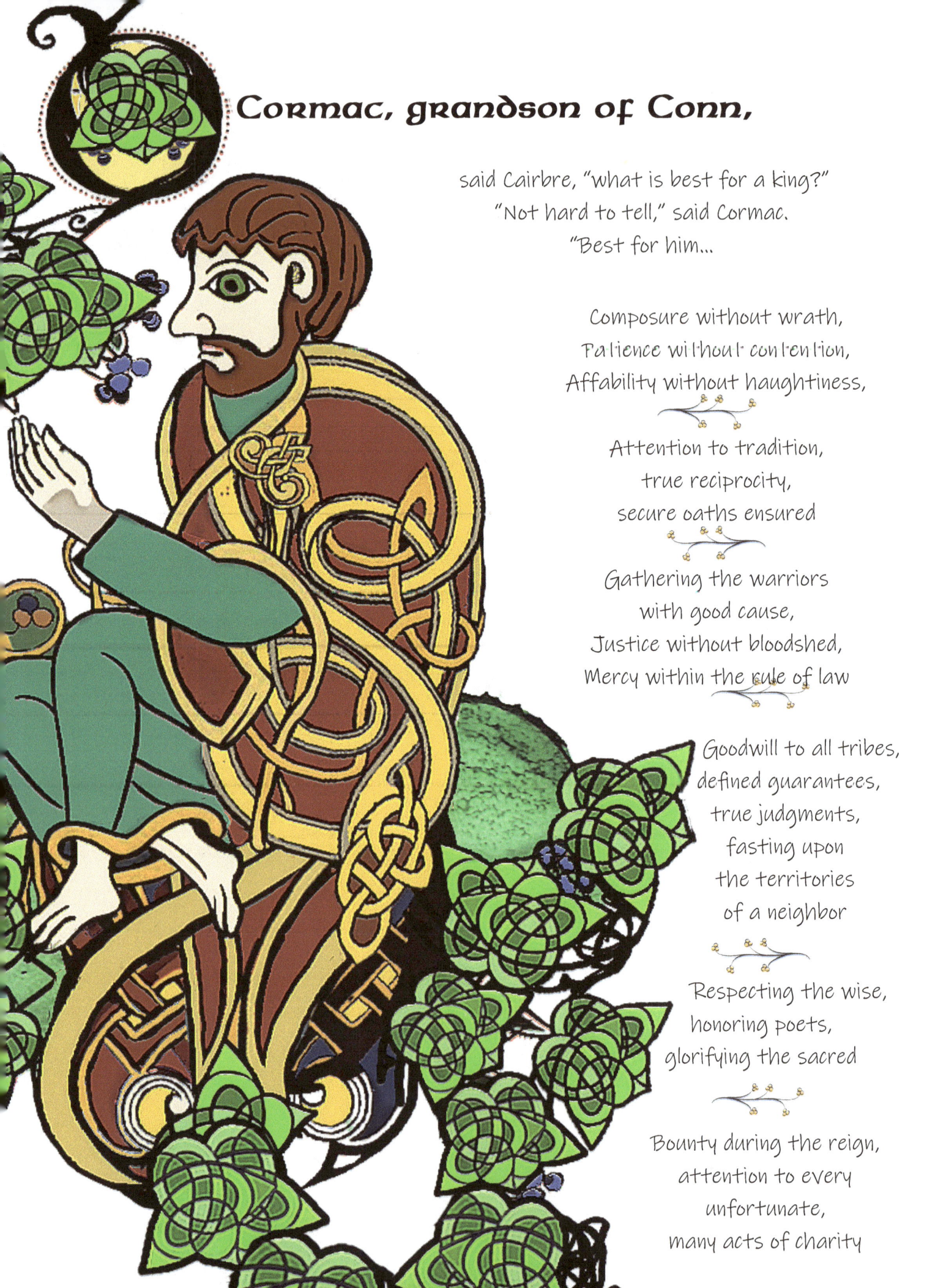

# Cormac, grandson of Conn,

said Cairbre, "what is best for a king?"
"Not hard to tell," said Cormac.
"Best for him...

Composure without wrath,
Patience without contention,
Affability without haughtiness,

Attention to tradition,
true reciprocity,
secure oaths ensured

Gathering the warriors
with good cause,
Justice without bloodshed,
Mercy within the rule of law

Goodwill to all tribes,
defined guarantees,
true judgments,
fasting upon
the territories
of a neighbor

Respecting the wise,
honoring poets,
glorifying the sacred

Bounty during the reign,
attention to every
unfortunate,
many acts of charity

Fruit on the trees,
fish in the waters,
Fertility on the land

Inviting ships into harbor,
rich goods imported,
shelter given to the waifs of the sea

A raiment of silk,
A troop to defend every tribe,
A skill in raiding parties

Let him attend the ailing,
let him aid the poor

Let him speak truth, let him rebuke falsehood

Let him love justice, let him quell fear

Let him crush criminals,, let him give true judgments

Let him know true value, let him improve his soul

Let him foster every branch of learning,
let there be an abundance of wine and mead,
let him strengthen every alliance

Let him declare every judgment clearly, let him speak every truth

For it is through the truth of the chieftain that God gives all!"

# Cormac, grandson of Conn,

said Cairbre, "Who is the worst protector?"

"Easy enough," said Cormac.

"A protector of little dignity
is one who sells his honor.
He puts up for sale his support,
His hand,
His breast,
His heart,
The dignity of his clan,
His people,
And himself

He makes no amends,
His compensations are empty,
His character is fickle,
His amity is short-lived

His protection is meager,
His claims are greater
than his abilities

He is the image
of a laughing stock
to all the folk.
He cannot raise his head,
wherever he may go or be."

# Cormac, grandson of Conn,

"what is the true power of leadership?"

"Not hard to tell. The power that rules upon the peaceful land,
that I have. Let me make it known to you."

Let him restrain the powerful,
Let him slay the evil,
Let him raise up the good

Let him subdue the outlaw,
Let him route the thief,
Let him establish order
among the folk

Let him nurture peace,
Let him plant law,
Let him root out unlawfulness,
Let him shackle the wicked,
Let him free the innocent

Let him protect the just,
Let him bind the unjust

Let him proclaim it so that all robbers shall know:
There shall be full liability for all those responsible
All fines shall be upon them

All penalties upon those who aided and knew of the crime,
Half the penalties upon those who aided without knowing

With the dignity of a king
And the duties of a leader,
Let him maintain the rights of all his folk,
whether on sea or land,
And with respect to what is the possession
of each tribe by right.

In regard to crimes,
whether they be of the hand,
Going about of feet,
Looking of eyes,
Misdeeds of the tongue,
Or of the ears,
With tests of conscience,
Let him clarify and attend to the rights of all.
Let him bring everyone together
under the law

And this is the right and the duty,
the power of leadership among the tribes!"

# Cormac, grandson of Conn,

said Cairbre, "what is the worst discourse?"
"Not hard to tell," said Cormac.

"Contending against knowledge,
Resorting to bad language,
Many insults,
Contention with no proof

stiffness of delivery,
Incompetence,
Forgetfulness

Muttering,
Clumsy delivery,
Speaking over others

Intellectual hair-splitting,
unestablished proof,
despising books,

turning against tradition,
talking in too loud a voice,
Asking for one thing and then another

inciting the multitude,
fighting everyone,
Pompous vanity,
Screaming at the judge,
Swearing after judgment."

"And what is the
worst request in court?"

"Not hard.
An angry, long-winded plea,
An unstable plea,
An empty, venting suit

Rapid, forgetful argument,
Incitement to offense,
Urges to violence
Playing games with
the favor of the folk,
Swearing hasty, reckless oaths,
Loud answers

Disturbing the assembly,
Snide and slanderous words,
Heavy-handedness."

# Cormac, grandson of Conn,

said Cairbre, "What are the qualities of a lord?"
"Not hard to tell," said Cormac.

"Let him honor geasa
Let him have self-mastery
Let him be a man of vigor
Let his desires be wholesome

Let him be of good will
Let him be affable
Let him be humble

Let him be quick
Let him be firm
Let him be a poet
Let him be wise
Let him know the laws

Let him be generous
Let him be genial
Let him be tender

Let him show that
law must be obeyed
Let him show mercy

him be perceptive
Let him be constant
Let him be patient
Let him be moderate

Let him teach the strong to aid the weak,
Let him give justice
Let him feed every orphan

Let him quell the wrong
Let him despise the lie
Let him love the truth
Let him forget the foolish slight
Let him remember the kindness

Let him be attended by many in gatherings
Let him be attended by few in counsel

Let him shine in the company
Let him be the sun in the mead-hall
Let his hall be opened often to host the folk

Let him be a lover of knowledge
Let him be a scrounge of evils
Let him remind all of their duty

Let him give each person their due,
Let him be a judge of every soul in the light of their place in life.

Let him pay liberal honors
to those of learning, skill and craft

Let his pledges be sure
Let his enforcement be lenient
Let his judgements be sharp and bright
For it is by those qualities kings and lords are judged,"

# Warnings of King Cormac to Cairbre:

Don't threaten a king,
Don't consort with a fool,
Don't associate with a bully,
Don't consort with a criminal

Don't race a chariot on foot
Don't stand where a spear is aimed
Don't set yourself against the mountain,
Don't try to fight the tide,
Don't walk foolishly into peril

Don't join in slander,
Don't play the fool in the gathering,
Don't grumble in the alehouse
Don't forget your promises,
Don't be argumentative,
Don't quarrel with the truth

Don't be a clever liar,
Don't aid a thief,
Don't start the argument

Don't be a thicket of strife,
Don't make a promise to a great many folk,
Don't promise what you don't have

Don't be a spendthrift, and you'll avoid debt
Don't be aggressive, and you'll avoid disgrace
Don't be argumentative, and you'll avoid animosity

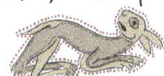

Don't be quarrelsome, and you won't get your head broken
Don't be rough, and you won't be a lout
Don't be combative, and you won't get your nose bloodied

Don't be absent, lest you be negligent
Don't be brusque, lest you be rude
Don't feed others so well that you become thin

Don't be lazy, lest that you lose your vigor,
Don't be over-eager, lest you make a fool of yourself
Don't be contentious, lest others cease to invite you in
Don't guarantee what you can't provide to your neighbors.

# Cormac, grandson of Conn,

'what were your deeds when you were a young man?'
'Not hard to tell,' said Cormac.

I would kill a boar and follow a track when I was alone,

I would march against a band of five when I was in a band of five,

I was ready to kill when I was in a band of ten,

I was ready to raid when I was in a band of twenty,

I was ready to give battle when I was in a band of a hundred

these were my deeds,' said Cormac to Cairbre.

# Cormac, grandson of Conn,

said Cairbre, "what is the basis of ridicule among the Irish?"
"Not hard to tell," said Cormac

"A man arrogant in his wisdom, his gifts, or his good fortune,

A man who is foppish, prideful, vainglorious

A man who is lazy, irascible, distractible

A man who is thoughtless, foolish, boastful

A man who is violent, argumentative, overbearing

A man who is stingy, unreliable, jealous

A man who is corrupt, stingy, easily offended

A man who is hasty, uncaring, tactless

A man who is churlish, senseless, demanding."

# Cormac, grandson of Conn,

"O Cormac, grandson of Conn," said Cairbre, "what is best for me?"
"Not hard to tell," said Cormac, "This is what I have to teach,"

"Do not scorn the elderly, though you be young,

nor the poor, though you be rich,

nor the naked, though you be finely-dressed

nor the lame, though you be fleet,

nor the blind, though you be keen of sight,

nor the weak, though you be strong,

nor the dull, though you be clever,

nor the fool, though you be wise.

Be not sluggish,

♦

be not irascible,

♦

be not slothful,

♦

be not stingy,

♦

be not idle,

♦

be not jealous.

♦

for the sluggish, the irascible,
the slothful, the stingy,
the idle and the jealous,
and before them all the one who scorns;
these are hateful before God
and society."

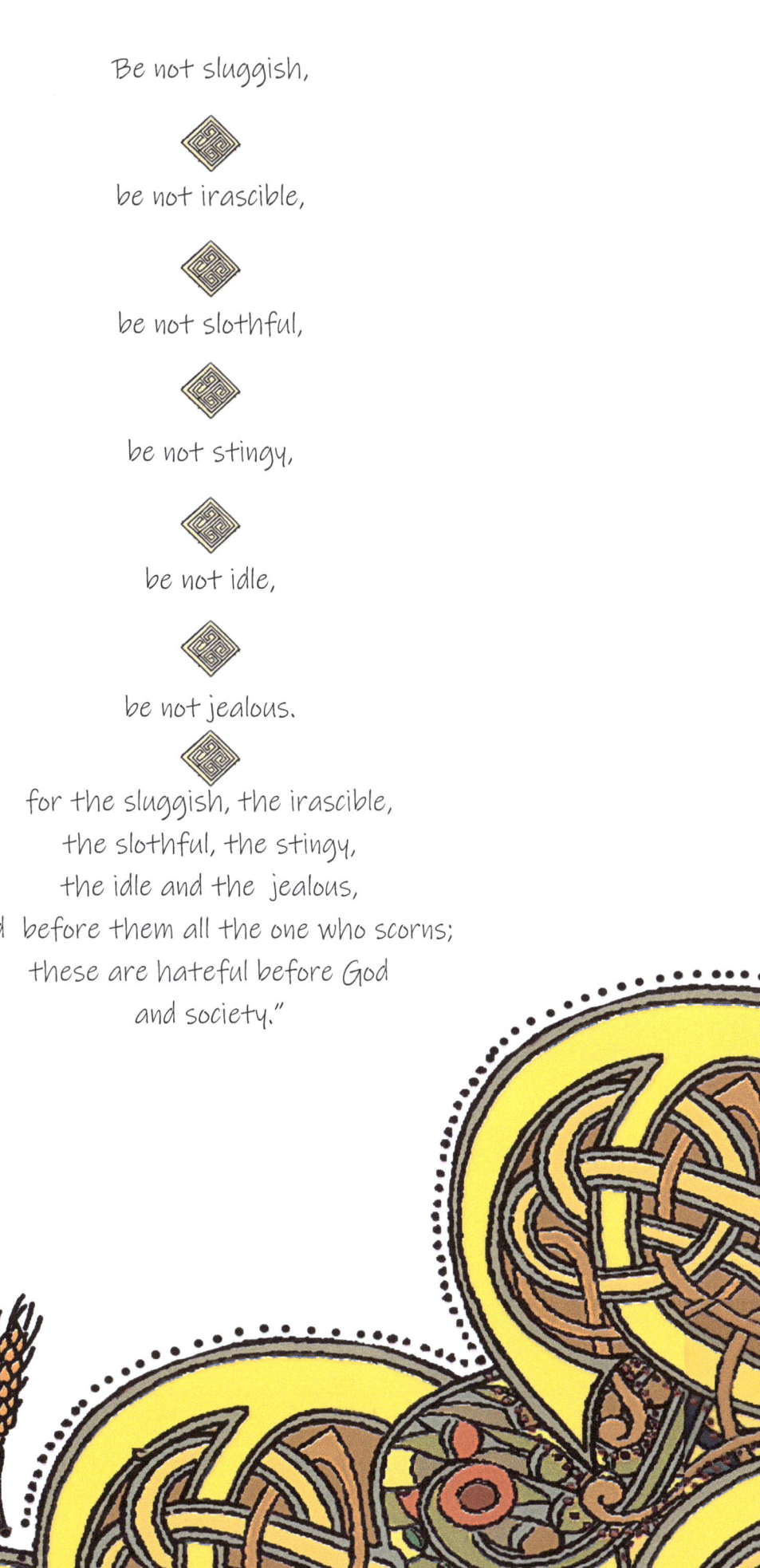

# Cormac, grandson of Conn,

said Cairbre, "What is worst for the human body?"
'Not hard to tell," said Cormac.

"Sitting too long,
lying too long,
being inactive,

heavy lifting,
Overexertion,
Loneliness

Too much running,
Too much leaping,
Too much clumsiness

Sleeping with a leg over the bed rail,
Seating a fast horse too often,
Staring at fire,
Walking in the dark,

Hot wax,
beestings,
new ale

Bull-flesh,
Curdled milk
dry food

bog-water,
rising too early
cold,
sun,
hunger,

Drinking much,
eating much,
sleeping much,
sinning much,

Melancholy,
running uphill,

shouting into the wind,
a blow beyond one's strength,
drying oneself by a fire,

summer-dew,
Winter-dew,
beating ashes,

swimming with a full belly,
Lying flat to sleep,
Gulping the drink,

frenzy,
foolhardiness."

# Cormac, grandson of Conn,

said Cairbre, "What is best for me?"
"Not hard to tell," said Cormac.

If you heed my advice,
you will not trade your honor
for ale or food.
It is better to save one's good name than to save one's food

Don't be proud unless you are a land-owner

Don't keep mares without stallions

Don't give feasts without first brewing ale

Be sparing with the milk unless you have cattle

Don't dress finely if you have no sheep

For pride without production,
luxury without husbandry,
entertainment without work,
drinking the milk without raising the cow,
fine dress without feeding the sheep

These things are a crime
against the folk of the world."

# Cormac, grandson of Conn,

said Cairbre, "the ways of folly,
what is their number?'
'Not hard to tell,' said Cormac.

"Swearing after a legal ruling,
Hasty decisions,
Rousing anger,

Lying whispers,
Cruel truths,
A failure of piety

Recanting a judgment given,
Sour words at a feast,
Lying words from the mouth of a chief

Mocking the elders,
Misrepresenting history,
Dancing on a cliff

Shooting without a target,
Competing with those who cannot stand against you,
Haughtiness with those who are owed respect

Failure to honor the law,
Performance of wrongs,
Doing disservice to friends
Betrayal to lovers,
Enchantment with passing novelties,
Contempt for the traditional

Action without evidence,
Incompetence in one's responsibilities,
Paying to sway legal decisions

Wasting what is gained,
Lending too much,

Counting friends by number rather than value
Grumbling and groaning at the King,
Much talk with little reason.

"These are the ways of folly," said Cormac.

**Cormac, grandson of Conn,** said Cairbre, "what do you deem the best and worst things you have seen?"
"Not hard to tell," said Cormac.

"The worst thing I have seen?
Faces of the enemy
Arrayed against me
On the field of war."

"Now, the best thing I have seen?
A gathering in song after victory
Praises given with just reward
A lady's invitation to adore her."

# Cormac, grandson of Conn, said Cairbre,

"What distinguishes the people of our race?"
"Not hard to tell," said Cormac.
"I distinguish them all, both
men, women, sons, and daughters."
"How is that?" Cairbre asked. Cormac said:

One who is steadfast is wise,
One who is generous is blessed,
One who is patient will persevere

One who is studious learns much,
One who loves the family is gentle,
One who is healthy is cheerful

One who is rash is a laughing stock,
One who is in bondage is gloomy,
One who is poor is proud

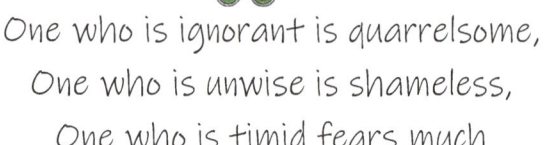

One who is ignorant is quarrelsome,
One who is unwise is shameless,
One who is timid fears much

One who is haunted by fear is cautious
One who is pleased by fear is cruel
One who is starving will steal

One who knows illness is honest,
One who knows suffering is compassionate,
One who carries anxieties is afflicted

One who is contentious is often in court
One who is full of life
loves the belling of the hounds on the hunt
One who is full of love
spends much time in the marital bed

A landlord is rich,
A craftsman is versatile,
A good man is generous

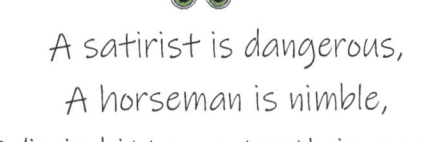

A satirist is dangerous,
A horseman is nimble,
A lie is bitter, a truth is sweet

The skillful woman is sweet-tongued
The ill-favored woman is venomous
Ill-met are her sons,
a sorrow to him who meets them!

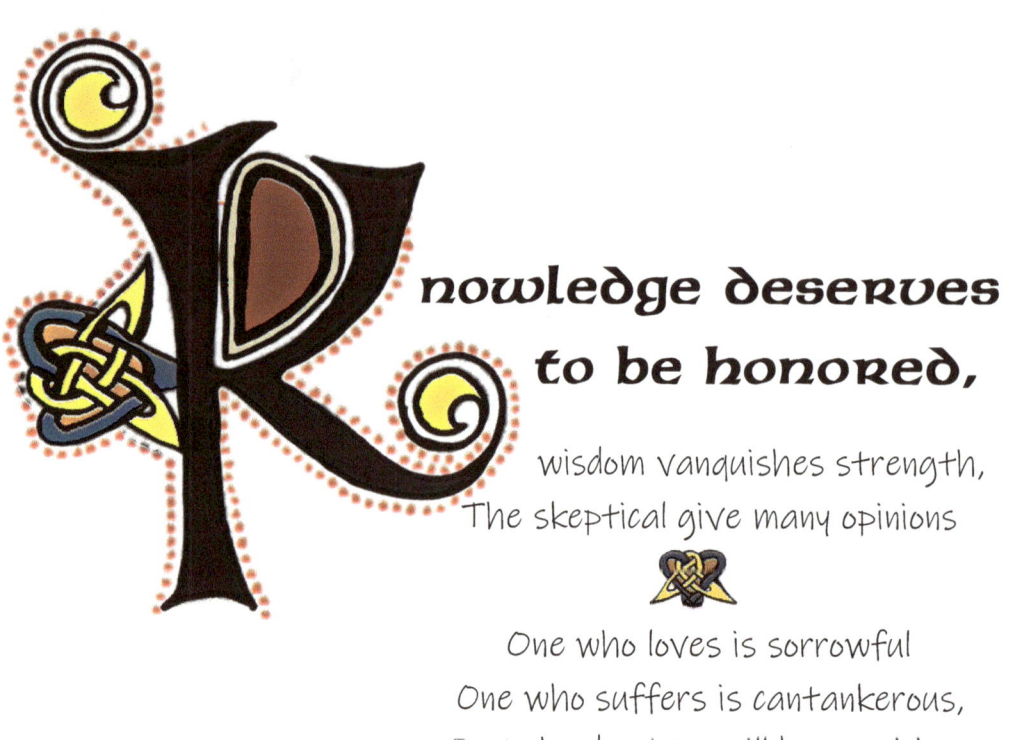

Knowledge deserves to be honored, wisdom vanquishes strength, The skeptical give many opinions

One who loves is sorrowful
One who suffers is cantankerous,
One who deceives will be suspicious

A fool is dangerous
A blowhard is in peril,
A fighter is ready to brawl

A good farmer is full of prudence,
A bad warrior is full of fury,
A covetous man is empty of shame

A danger is dreadful
A darkness is fearful
A rent-bonded one hangs their head low

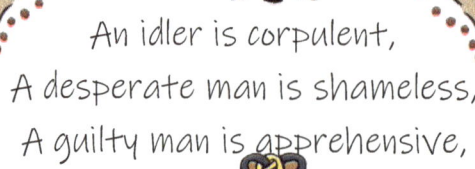

An idler is corpulent,
A desperate man is shameless,
A guilty man is apprehensive,

A mocking man is loud-voiced
A cautious man is quiet-voiced
An evil mind has a quarrelsome tongue

The cheerful man is fond of gatherings,
The good clan is fond of assembling,
The good king is fond of hosting

The litigious one grumbles,
The courageous one is gentle,
The violent one is remiss in their duties

One who tells the future is lying
One who wastes is a fool
One who is impatient is ridiculous

One who has power is in risk of being reviled,
One who shouts insults is a coward,
One who is well-disciplined is wise

One who is sensible is competent
One who is honest acknowledges rights
One who has known suffering is humane.

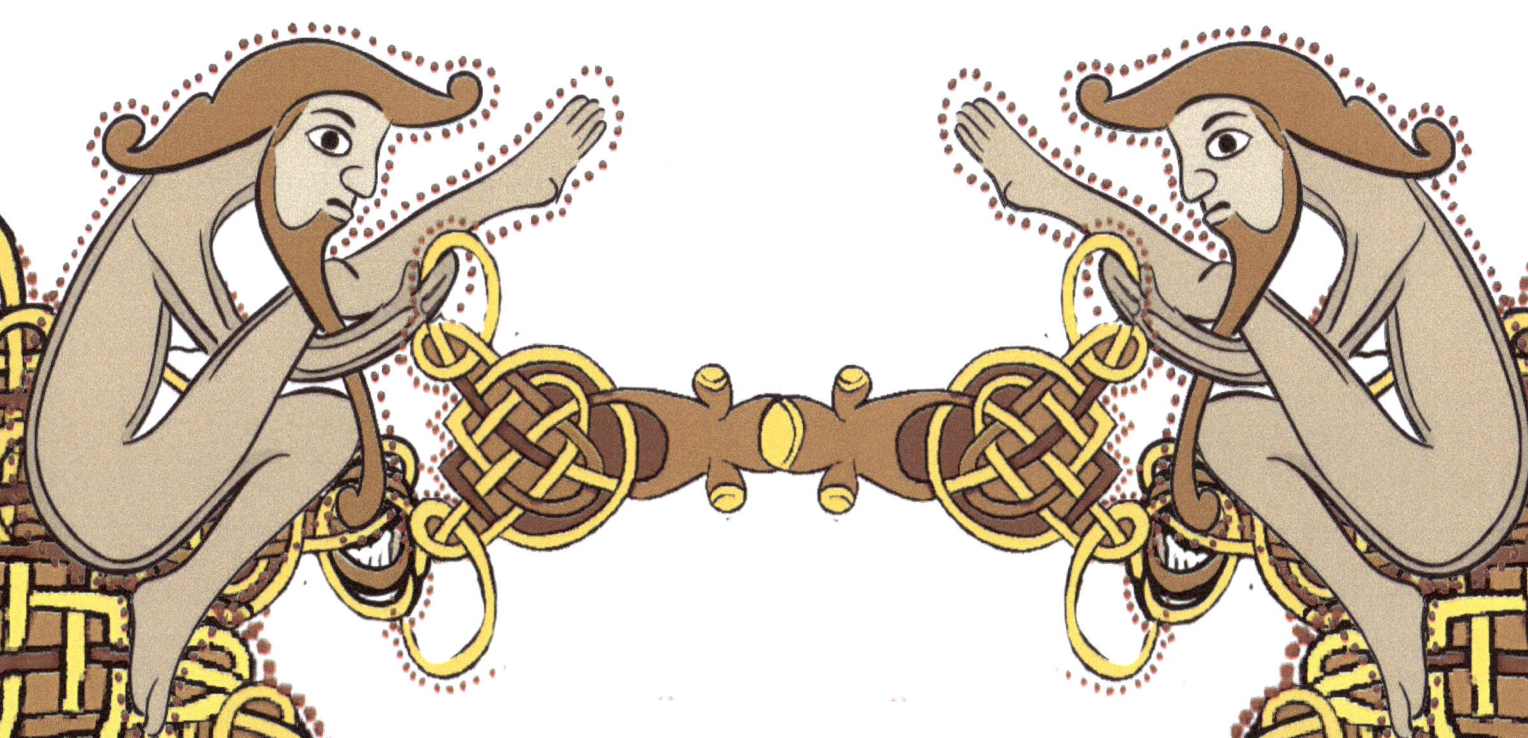

# Cormac, grandson of Conn,

said Cairbre, "what is fitting for both
a chieftain's hall and an ale house?"
"Not hard to tell," said Cormac,

"Affability in the company of worthy folk,

A well-lit place of many lanterns,

Good effort made to bring joy to the gathering,

A seat for every soul

A generous hand in giving,

A nimble hand in filling the bowls,

Readiness of supply

Loyalty and respect,

Pleasure balanced with good sense,

A story with no boast in it

A cheerful face,
Welcoming the poets,
Silence during the recitation of wisdom,
Strong voice in song with your fellows.

These things make both an ale-house
and a chieftain's hall good," said Cormac.

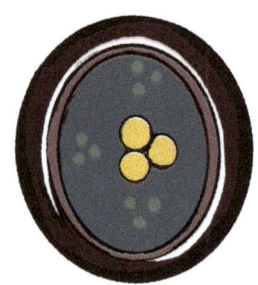# Cormac, grandson of Conn,

said Cairbre, "how does a chieftain show that he is worthy of his station?"

"Not hard to tell," said Cormac,

"It is gained by excellence:

Excellence of appearance

Excellence of gathering

Excellence of discernment

Excellence of family

Excellence of integrity

Excellence of eloquence

It is shown by the absence of outlaws,

It is shown by the presence of many friends."

 # Cormac, grandson of Conn,

said Cairbre, "What are the unworthy qualities
which you compare with these?"

"That's easy," said Cormac,

"The rough,
The bitter,
The rude,

The violent,
The vehement,
The vulgar,

The impetuous,
The forgetful,
The noisy,

The audacious,
Wise after the fact,

He who waits for no one, and who no one waits for,
He does not heed and is not heeded,
He is shunned by the folk and the faith.

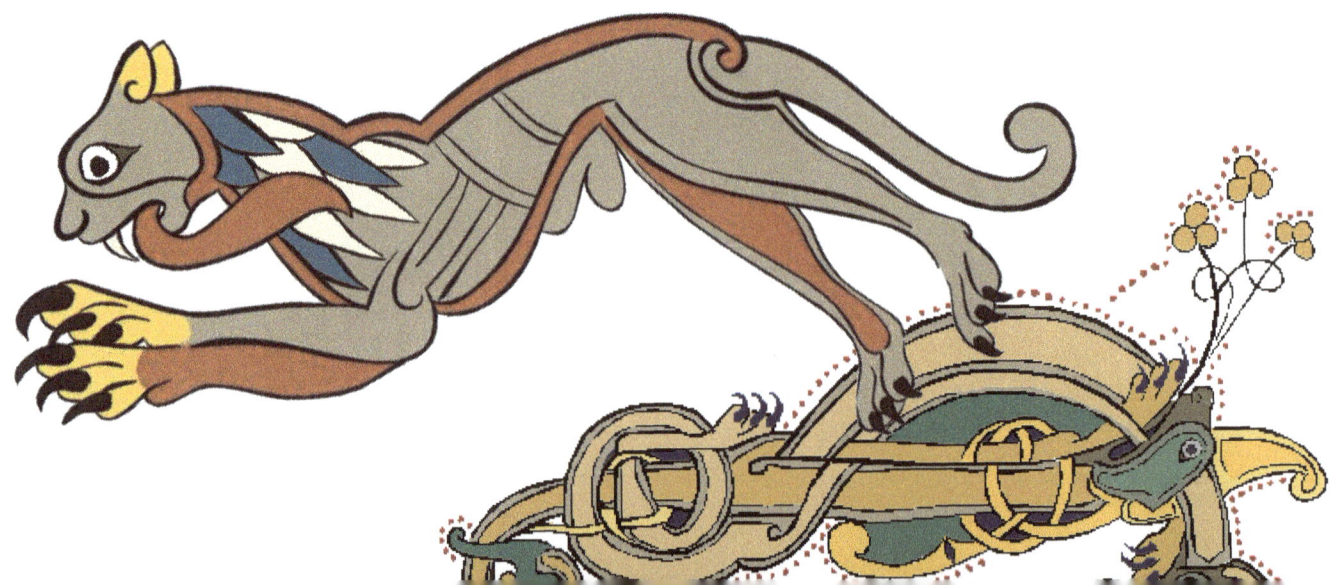

The shamelessness of a satirist,
With the memory of a historian

The integrity of a wretch,
Paired to the cunning of a cur,

The conscience of a dog,
with the hand of a thief,

The strength of a bull,
With the contentiousness of a lawyer,

The craftiness of a weasel,
With the speech of a wealthy man,

The habits of an heir,
With the oath of a horse thief

Shrewdness, deceit, hoarfrost-coldness, vehemence, a tongue for cursing.
And above all, an arrogant speech: "It is settled! I'll take an oath on it!"

# Cormac, grandson of Conn,

said Cairbre, "What is best for the seasons?"

"Easy enough,

Winter fine and frosty,

Spring dry and breezy,

Summer dry and showery,

Autumn dewy and fruitful."

"And how do you read the weathers?"

"Not hard to tell," said Cormac,

"Ice is mother to grain

Snow is father to bacon

Wet is forewarning of feud

Drought is promise of plague

Wind is troublesome in the straits,

the best of weathers is mist,

better his brother rain,

Thunder has no value,

Lest it be the thunder of the sea."

 **Cormac, grandson of Conn,**
"I wish to know how I shall behave
among the wise and the foolish,
among friends and strangers,
among the old and the young,
among the innocent and the wicked."

"Not hard to tell," said Cormac.

"Be not too wise, be not too foolish,

be not too conceited, be not too timid,

be not too haughty, be not too humble,

be not too talkative, be not too silent,

be not too harsh, be not too feeble.

Too wise, and expectations will be imposed on you

Too foolish, and you'll be duped

Too conceited, and you'll be devoid of friendship

Too timid, and you'll be robbed of dignity

Too talkative, and you'll be dismissed

Too silent, and you'll be disregarded

Too hard, and you'll be broken,

Too soft, and you'll be squashed."

**A** question, my father, said Cairbre, " "how should I be?"
"That's easy," said Cormac

Be knowledgeable to the learned,
So that you will not be duped

Be proud to the haughty,
So that you will not be made to quail

Be humble to the humble,
And your will shall be theirs

Be talkative with the talking,

So that you will be heard

Be silent with the quiet

So that you will be able to hear

Be hard with the harsh,

So that you will not be humiliated

Be soft with the soft

And bring no unkindness down upon you."

"O son, if you listen to me," said Cormac, "this is my counsel to you:

Do not let a man who owes favors be your steward,

Do not let a woman with sons and foster-sons be your housekeeper,

Do not let a covetous man manage your household,

Do not let a man of much delay be your miller,

Do not let a violent foul-mouthed man your messenger,

Do not let a grumbling sluggard be your servant,

Do not let a garrulous man be your confidant,

Do not let a heavy-drinking man be your cup-bearer,

Do not let a man with a bad eyes be your watchman,

Do not let a bitter, haughty man be your doorkeeper,

Do not let an indulgent man be your judge,

Do not let a man without knowledge your leader,

Do not let an unfortunate man be your advisor."

# Cormac, grandson of Conn,

said Cairbre, "Who do you consider deaf in the world?"

"Easy enough,

A doomed man being given a warning,

Someone being asked an unpleasant thing,

A gossip who is told to hush."

# Cormac, grandson of Conn,

said Cairbre, "What is lasting in the world?"

"Easily told," said Cormac.

"Grass

bronze,

a yew tree.

That is all."

# Notes on the Translation And Cultural Context of the Counsels

# Abhcóide Aon
# Alt a Seacht
# Tecosca Cormaic

'A húi Chuind, a Chormaic,' ol Carpre,
'cia bátar do bésa intan ropsa gilla?'
'Ní hansa,' ol Cormac.

Ba-sa coistechtach caille,
ba déscenach renda,
ba dall rúine,

ba tó fásaig,
ba labor sochuide,
ba shulig midchúarta,

ba dulig irgaile,
ba solam d'foraire,
ba cennais cairdine,

ba liaig lobor,
ba fann fri amnirt,
ba trén fri rúanaid,

nírba chrúaid ar ná ba áertha,
nírba timm ar ná ba maelchend,
nírba ocus ar ná ba tromm,
nírba labar ciapsa gácth,

nírba taircsinach ciarba trén,
nírba laimthenach ciarba lúath,
ní cuitbinn sen ciarba óc,
nírba moidmech ciarba gonach,

ní lúaidinn nech ina écmais,
ní aiscinn is nomolainn,
ní cuinginn is doberainn,

'ar is triasna
bésu sin rosegat óic
corbat sin & rígláich.'

# Counsel the First
# From Paragraph 7
# Counsels Of Cormac

"O Cormac, grandson of Conn,"
said Cairbre,
"What were your habits
when you were a lad?"
"Not hard to tell," said Cormac

I was a listener in the woods,
I was a gazer at the stars,
I was blind to men's secrets

I was silent in the wild places
I was talkative in the gathering
I was genial in the mead-hall
I was harsh in battle

I was kind in friendship,
I was a physician of the sick
I was gentle towards the feeble
I was strong against the powerful

I was not harsh, lest I should be satirized
I did not cling, lest I should be burdensome
I was not chattering, though I was clever
I was not arrogant, though I was wise

I was not boastful, though I was strong
I was not venturesome, though I was swift
I did not deride the old, though I was young
I was not bragging, though I was capable

I would not speak about another in his absence
I would not reproach, but I would praise
I would not ask, but I would give

For it is through these habits
that the young
grow strong and proud."

# Abhcóíde Dó
## Alt a Trí
### Tecosca Cormaic

'A húi Chuind, a Chormaic,' ol Carpre,
'cid as dech do less túathe?'
'Ní hansa,' ol Cormac.

Terchomrac dagdóine,
Dála menci,
Menma athchomairc,

Fochmarc do gáethaib,
Airdíbdud cech uilc,
Comalnad cech mathiusa,

10] Airecht ríaglach,
Sechem senchusa,
Senad rechtaide,

Rechtge la flaith,
Tóisech fíréna,
Cen forbrisiud trúag,
Comad chairddine,

Trócaire co ndagbésaib,
Dlúthugud coibniusa,
Comúaim coimgne,

Comalnad rechtge,
Recht senchairdde,
Cotach cen timdibe,

Fíanna cen díummus,
Inire fri náimtiu,
Indraccus fri bráthriu,

Rátha fíala,
Aithi slána,
Bretha fíra,

Folaid chutrummae,
Airlicud éim,
Géill do inchaib,

Íasacht follán,
Óin fri toich,
Cubés cach maith,

Taithesc míadchar,
Messair dílmain,
Foglaimm cach dána,

Eolas cech bérlai,
Druine mrechtrad,
Tacra co fásaigib,

Brithemnas co roscadaib,
Tabairt almsan,
Trócaire fri bochtu,

Gella fri bretha,
Nadmann indraicce,
Étsecht fri sruithi,

Buidre fri dáescarsluag,
Lessugud críche ar cach n-olc,
Ní ba réidenech oc less túaithe,
Ní ba gerthide i n-ailt midchúarto —

dech do les túathe in sin.

# Counsel the Second
## From Paragraph 3
## The Counsels of Cormac

"O Cormac, Grandson of Conn,"
said Cairbre, "what is best for the good of a tribe?"
"Not hard to tell," said Cormac.

"A gathering of good folk,
often taking counsel,
An inquiring mind,

Consulting the wise,
Quelling every evil,
Ensuring every good

Often holding court,
Following tradition,
Upholding law

A chieftain who leads justly,
A law that is administered fairly,
staving off the crushing of the weak

Keeping good relations,
Graciousness to the well-meaning,
Strengthening connections

Weaving learning into wisdom,
Keeping the law,
Authority of ancient alliances

Friendship without fickleness,
Strength without vainglory,
Showing integrity to foe and kin alike

Generous pledges,
complete repayment,
just rulings,
Honest witnesses,

Bargains kept honestly,
Interest on loss, Fair weights and fair measures,
Ready hiring for the season's work,
Promises offered in accordance with your station,

Lending without stint,
Loans for wholesome purposes,
An equivalent for every good;
A dignified response, legitimate measure

Studying every art,
Knowledge of every language,
Skill in many crafts,
Argumentation using legal precedents,
Passing judgment with wisdom

Giving alms t the poor,
giving justice, giving mercy,
Honest contracts

Attention to elders and dismissal to fools,
Never a forgetting of the needs of the folk
Never the chieftain at feast
when the people hunger—

These things are best for the good of the tribe."

**O**ne of the last lines in this piece is 'never a forgetting of the needs of the folk, never the chieftain at feast when the people hunger."

Originally, it ran:

'Ní ba rethide oc less túaithe, Ní ba gerthide i n-ailt midchúarto'
'Let him not be smooth-facedas far as the profit of the kingdom is concerned
Let him not be greasy in the house of the mead-court'

There's a wealth of cultural knowledge held in these words. In 9th century Ireland, getting a good shave and a clean haircut was valued, but it was also expensive; the blades required skill and care to use. Getting a shave was the equivalent of going to a fancy salon, in its day. And even today, we know how good greasy meat tastes. In those days, it wasn't common. A good cut of fat meat was the filet mignon of the time.

It's wonderful that in these ancient works, one of the reminders to leaders is 'don't let your people see you fancied up and eating well when you haven't fulfilled your responsibilities.'

# Abhcóide Trí
## Alt Tríocha a haon
### Tecosca Cormaic

Cormac beos roráid inso:
Gáeth cách co reic a forbbai,
báeth cách co lóg tíre,
cara cách co fíachu,
rechtaid cách co lelbu,
súanach cách co clemnas,
ferach cách co cresine,
sochlu cách co áir,
brugaid cách co eitech,
fénnid cách co trebad,
amos cách co árus,
sochonn cách co meisci,
codnach cách co feirg,
sognaid cách co fuichecht,
sobraig cách co altrom,
rúnaid cách co ugra,
urraid cách co fócra,
fáilid cách co dona,
dána cách co hetech,
troigthech cách co cairptech,
cáid cách ceól co cruit,
sochraid cách sona,
dochraid cách dona,
milsem codalta freislige,
milsem cormae cétdeoch,
milsem ceól ceól i ndoirche,
milsem lochta airigid
Duine óc sochoisc umal erlataid bus léir cubus & cobais,
bid cóem a óitiu, bid sruith a sentu,
bid fír a briathar, bid cáid a forgnúis,
bid úasal cid ísel,
bid sen cid óc,
bid maith a forcenn la Día & duine.'

# Counsel The Third
## From Paragraph 31
## The Counsels Of Cormac

Of the folk, Cormac said to Cairbre:
Everyone is wise till he sells his inheritance,
everyone is foolish till he buys land,
everyone is a friend till it comes to debts,
everyone is a judge till it comes to children,
everyone is slothful till it comes to marrying,
everyone is rowdy till it comes to religion,
everyone is respected till he is satirized,
everyone is hospitable till he turns one from the door,
everyone is a roving warrior till he takes up farming,
everyone is a servant till he settles in his own home,
everyone is sound of mind till he drinks spirits,
everyone is sensible till he is roused,
everyone is decorous till he commits adultery,
everyone is tranquil till he has children,
everyone is confident till he begins to quarrel,
everyone is a citizen till he is denounced,
everyone is cheerful till he meets with bad luck,
everyone is bold till he meets with a refusal.
One is a pedestrian till he drives a chariot,
One who prospers has dignity
One who suffers illness has shame
The sweetest sleep is in lying together
The sweetest ale is in the first draught
The sweetest music is the music in the dark
The sweetest person is the worthy one
A young person who keeps these things in mind
will be lovable in youth,
venerable in age,
true in word,
honorable in appearance.
If he is amiable, humble, obedient,
earnest in word and deed,
then he will be respected in spite of his station,
he will be wise in spite of his years,
and his future will be assured with God and folk.'

The oblique humor that is so characteristic of this work shines in these words. Lines such as 'everyone is respected till he is satirized,' or 'everyone is sound of mind till he drinks spirits,' will make a modern reader smile in rueful commiseration. In these words, we can recognize ourselves at our most buffoonish.

Along with a chance to smile, we're also given a reminder to have compassion for others in our community: where that person you're looking down on might be today, you might be tomorrow. After all, everyone is doing well…until they're not.

The most interesting thing about this work is the post-script, beginning with the words 'A young person who keeps these things in mind…' which in the original work seems to have been written at a later date, possibly by a different scribe. If that is the case, it makes the modern scholar wonder whether the later hand was trying to 'rectify' the cheeky element in the verses above.

## Abhcóide Ceathair
## Alt a Aon
## Tecosca Cormaic

'A húi Chuind, a Chormaic,'
ol Carpre, 'cid as dech do ríg?'
'Ní hansa,' ol Cormac. 'Dech dó,

Fosta cen feirg,
Ainmne cen debaid,
Soacallaim cen mórdataid,

Deithide senchasa,
Frithfolad fír,
Géill i nglassaib,

Slógad fri deithbiri,
Fír cen fuillem,
Trócaire co ndlúthugud rechta,

Síd do thúathaib,
Rátha écsamla,
Bretha fíra,
Troscud for cocrichaib,

Mórad nemed,
Airmitiu filed,
Adrad De móir,
Torud inna flaith,
Deicsiu cach thrúaig,

Almsana ile,
Mess for crannaib,
Íasc i n-inberaib,
Talam torthech,

Bárca do thochor i port,
Allmaire sét,
Murchuirthe dílse,

Étach sirecda,
Drong claidebbémnech ar choimét cacha túaithe,
Forrana dar crícha,

Torramad lubru,
Lessaiged triunu,

Techtad fír,
Cairiged gói,

Carad fírinni,
Dinged oman,

Báded bidbadu,
Bered fírbretha,

Bíathad cech n-ái,
Uaged cach síd,
Criad máine,

Lessaiged anmain
Aisnéided cach réilbreth,

Imbed fína sceo meda,
Canad cach fír,

ar is tria fír flaitheman dobeir Día in sin uile.'

# Counsel The Fourth
# From Paragraph 1,
# The Counsels Of Cormac

"O Cormac, grandson of Conn," said Cairbre,
"what is best for a king?"
"Not hard to tell," said Cormac.
"Best for him…
Composure without wrath,
Patience without contention,
Affability without haughtiness,

Attention to tradition,
true reciprocity,
secure oaths ensured

Gathering the warriors with good cause,
Justice without bloodshed,
Mercy within the rule of law

Goodwill to all tribes,
defined guarantees,
true judgments,
fasting upon the territories of a neighbor

Respecting the wise,
honoring poets,
glorifying the sacred

Bounty during the reign,
attention to every unfortunate,
many acts of charity

Fruit on the trees,
fish in the waters,
Fertility on the land

Inviting ships into harbor,
rich goods imported,
shelter given to the waifs
of the sea

A raiment of silk,
A troop to defend every tribe,
A skill in raiding parties

Let him attend the ailing,
let him aid the poor

Let him speak truth,
Let him rebuke falsehood

Let him love justice,
let him quell fear

Let him crush criminals,
Let him give true judgments

Let him know true value,
let him improve his soul

Let him foster every branch of learning,
let there be an abundance of wine and mead,
let him strengthen every alliance

Let him declare every judgment clearly,
let him speak every truth

For it is through the truth of the chieftain
that God gives all!"

# Abhcóide Cúig
## Alt Tríocha Trí
### Tecosca Cormaic

'A húi Chuind, a Chormaic,' ol Carpre,
'cia mesam comairge?'
'Ní hansa,' ol Cormac.
'Comairge béldub becenech
renas a grúaid
a glún
a lám
a chích
a chride
fír a chlainde
a cheneóil & a gaisced.
Is lomm a díre,
is toll a eneclann,
is prap a persannacht,
is gerr a chuire,
is seng a snádugud,
ní lugu a lám nách a ordan,
is fúathledb genaige a delb fiad cach duine,
is cuitbide cennísel sechip maigen imté & i mbé.'

## Counsel the Fifth
## From Paragraph 33,
## The Counsels Of Cormac

"O Cormac, grandson of Conn," said Cairbre,
"Who is the worst protector?"
"Easy enough," said Cormac.
"A protector of little dignity is one who sells his honor.
He puts up for sale his support,
His hand,
His breast,
His heart,
The dignity of his clan,
His people,
And himself
He makes no amends,
His compensations are empty,
His character is fickle,
His amity is short-lived
His protection is meager,
His claims are greater than his abilities
He is the image of a laughing stock to all the folk
He cannot raise his head, wherever he may go or be."

**W**here the first few Counsels were mainly directed at how a person should act or in how they are by nature, later in the text the writing becomes quite pointed about how a person in Old Irish society should *not* act.

The use of the term 'protector' here is interesting. The modern Irish 'cosain' comes from the Old Irish root word consní; to strive for or to cost. This root shows the relationship of protection and care for someone in accordance with the communal standards codified in the Brehon Laws: to be the protector of someone is to pay for their mistakes.

This focus on reparation and the need to see things balanced out in society is also reflected a few lines later, where the poor protector's lack of amends and poor compensations are mentioned. 'His compensations are empty' can be interpreted in two ways: it could mean that when verbal amends are made they can't be trusted, or it could mean that, literally, the protector in question does not deliver eric, a word that translates best as 'reparation in the form of goods for wrongs done'. By the standards of the day, that would make a very poor protector indeed, whether that be a foster parent, a person responsible for the affairs of a community, or a king. For this reason, the illustration features a yelling man and rats being chased by terriers, in images based on examples from the Book of Kells.

Interesting research has been done on the rat in Irish art: when it appears, it symbolizes 'quiet crimes', covert actions such as embezzlement. This association came about very naturally: early Irish culture relied heavily on barley as a staple food. Wheat did not grow quite as well in the country, but it was popular enough to be grown and stored as well. In prehistoric times, the Irish dug a bell-shaped pit to store their grain. Once the community had filled it at harvest time, they placed a large clay cap over the hole in order to seal out air, light and excess moisture.

The grain that contacts the soil germinated, using up the existing oxygen and forming a barrier around the rest of the grain, which would fail to germinate and remain perfectly preserved. This method could conceivably store grain for several years, but it wasn't particularly reliable. Later people began to build wood or stone granaries, but that brought in new problems: mice and rats would enter around the foundations of the building and eat an incredible amount of grain. By the time a community looked in the grain store around the dark of winter, it would be seriously depleted and contaminated with droppings.

Given this association, rats and mice became the symbol of a small evil that destroys large endeavors. Keep an eye out for mice and rats in the margins as you study Irish manuscripts: when you see them, know that the original artist intended you to think of creeping malice and hidden wrongdoings.

These words were written in accordance with a very specific law system governing a particular culture. Yet they do resonate today, and the words are surprisingly relevant.
What makes a poor leader?
One whose words you can't trust.
One who acts only out of transactional need, not out of integrity and duty.
This is true throughout the ages.

# Abhcóide Sí
# Alt a Dó
# Tecosca Cormaic

'A húi Chuind, a Chormaic,' ol Carpre,
'cate cóir rechta ríg?'
'Ní hansa.
Recht fallnathar for talman tuind,
atáthum, atchous duit,'

Congbad máru,
Marbad ulcu,
Mórad maithi,

Tróethaid foglaide,
Argaired gait,
Córaigid coibnius,

Comúaiged síd,
Clandad dliged,
Cosced indliged,
Dóeraid bidbadu,
Sóerad enngu,

Anced idnu,
Cuimriged essidnu,

Fócraid foglaide:
Lándílse do cach láim la fíachu,
Comláithre lánfíachaib fis,
lethfiachaib,
anfis,

Co cátu ríg,
Co fursmaltaib flatha,
Conóiged dliged téchta
cech fír do neoch as leis muir & tír,
Foltaib fíraib do thúathaib
ata lais cintaib láime,

Forimthecht coss,
Silliud súla,
cintaib bél,
Étsecht clúas,
Co fíraib cuibse,
Lérigider cert cech cind,

Timmoirged cách fo recht,
ar it é téchta flatha in sin fri túatha!

# Counsel the Sixth
## From Paragraph 2,
## The Counsels Of Cormac

"O Cormac, grandson of Conn," said Cairbre,
"what is the true power of leadership?"

"Not hard to tell.
The power that rules upon the peaceful land,
that I have.
Let me make it known to you."

Let him restrain the powerful,
Let him slay the evil,
Let him raise up the good

Let him subdue the outlaw,
Let him route the thief,
Let him establish order among the folk

Let him nurture peace,
Let him plant law,
Let him root out unlawfulness,
Let him shackle the wicked,
Let him free the innocent

Let him protect the just,
Let him bind the unjust

Let him proclaim it so that all robbers shall know:
There shall be full liability for all those responsible

All fines shall be upon them
All penalties upon those
who aided and knew of the crime,
Half the penalties upon those who aided
without knowing

With the dignity of a king
And the duties of a leader,
Let him maintain the rights of all his folk,
whether on sea or land,
And with respect to what is
the possession of each tribe by right.

In regard to crimes,
Whether they be of the hand,
Going about of feet,
Looking of eyes,
Misdeeds of the tongue,
Or of the ears,
With tests of conscience,
Let him clarify and attend to the rights of all.

Let him bring everyone together
under the law

And this is the right and the duty,
the power of leadership among the tribes!"

This is a very classic and common-sense counsel, simply stating the work of good rulers throughout time: to listen to their people, care for the community's safety, their dignity, and ensure their health. But one passage brings up a particularly enlightening element of Irish law.

In the passage beginning with 'let him proclaim it so that all robbers shall know', Cormac discusses criminal law in terms of both knowledge and proportionality. This is an integral element of Irish law known as einachlan, or 'reparations for crimes against dignity', usually translated as honor-price.
What is interesting in the workings of the Irish law is in its function: rather than being focused on punishment, Brehon law was focused on restitution and reparations in all civil matters. What is particularly fascinating is that, in this section, Cormac's words stress a very modern sense of proportionality and intent: an unwitting criminal paid only half the penalties to the damaged party. If someone was tricked into, say, carrying a bag full of stolen goods for a friend, he would pay a half-fine for being what we, in modern law, would call an unwitting accomplice. Given that the law of most of continental Europe at the time did not consider the knowledge or intent of the criminal to be admissible in court, this is an incredible element of law for its time.

## Abhcóide Seacht
## Alt Fíche a Dó-Fíche a Cuíg
## Tecosca Cormaic

'A húi Chuind, a Chormaic,' ol Carpre,
'cia messam tacra & fuigell?'
'Ní hansa,' ol Cormac.
'Secht comartha deac drochthacra:

Frithchathugud fessa,
attach ndrochbérlai,
ilar n-athise,
cathugud cen chomartha,

rigne labartha,
folabra n-indsci,
imscoltad ngáise,

derbad n indorb,
dínsem lebar,
sóud fri nóisi,

roairde ngotha,
útmaille tacrai,
sprecad sochuide,

cathugud cáich,
a adbchlos fadéin,
grécha cinn,
luga iar mbreith.
'

'A báis, a dermatche,
'Ái lugach, ái móeth mall rigin.'

'cia mesam ái airechta?'
'Ní hansa,

Ái lonn lenamuach fota,
ái útmaille,
toiched toll telachtach,

tacra dían dermatach,
dúscad ferge,
fordinge forlonn,

báide báeglaige,
luige lúatha laimthecha,
frecra n-ard n-óbéle,

búaidred n-airechta,
ainme mbréithre,
lám do sund.

## Counsel the Seventh:
## From Paragraphs 22-25
## The Counsels Of Cormac

"O Cormac, Grandson of Conn," said Cairbre,
"what is the worst discourse?"
"Easy enough," said Cormac,
"There are seventeen manners of bad discourse:

Contending against knowledge,
Resorting to bad language,
Many insults,
Contention with no proof

stiffness of delivery,
Incompetence,
Forgetfulness

Muttering,
Clumsy delivery,
Speaking over others

Intellectual hair-splitting,
unestablished proof,
despising books,

turning against tradition,
talking in too loud a voice,
Asking for one thing and then another

inciting the multitude,
fighting everyone,
Pompous vanity,
Screaming at the judge,
Swearing after judgment."

"And what is the worst request in court?"
"Not hard.

An angry, importunate,
long-winded plea
An unstable plea,
An empty, venting suit

Rapid, forgetful argument,
Incitement to offense,
Urges to violence
Playing games with the favor of the folk,
Swearing hasty, reckless oaths,
Loud answers

Disturbing the assembly,
Snide and slanderous words,
Heavy-handedness."

For the Irish people in Cormac's day, good discourse—what we would call rhetorical skill today—was one of the signs of education. Culturally, there are many reasons for this. This being a time when there were no microphones, no cameras, and few technological embellishments for the human voice, a person who intended to be heard in assemblies had to speak up and speak well. Not only did they have to remember their speech, but they had to speak it in a way that allowed the whole room to hear and, hopefully, be moved by the words. The importance of good speech and good manners is emphasized again and again in period writings.

This incomplete Irish passage from the work Mittelirische Verslehren by Rudolf Thurneysen is a perfect example. It's drawn from a copy of the Auraicept na n-Éces, The Scholar's Primer as it's known in English, and names a number of formats for poetry, as well as general good conventions of trained speech and education for a fili in training. I've left the Irish in the state that Mr. Thurneysen penned it, but I've updated the translation slightly for readability.

In hí dā foglaim na hochtmaide bliadna .i. fi scomarca fi led .i.
duili berla 7
clethchor choem 7
reicne roscadach 7 laíde .i. tenmlaída 7
immas forosnai 7
dichetal do chennaib na tuaithe 7 dínshenchus 7
primscéla Hérend olchena fria naisnéis do ríghaib 7 fl aithib 7 dagdhoínib.
Ar ni comlán ín fi li chena, sicut dixit poeta:
Nibadúnad cenrígu. nibafi li censcéla.
níbaingen manibfi al. nímaith ciall neich natléga.

These are what are taught
in the eighth year: the tokens of wisdom of the fili;
the elements of language, the fair palisade
the poetic rhapsody,
A third type, the pithy work,
The work of great wisdom that enlightens
The work of naming the heads of the tribe.
In the eighth year is learned
Place-name lore
And the great tales of Ireland besides,
which are of the kings, princes, and nobles.
For a poet is not complete without these things,
A fort is no fort without kings;
a fili is no fili without tales;
a girl is no girl if she is not modest;
the intelligence of one who does not read is not good.

In addition, though literacy was surprisingly common for this time period in the country of Ireland, there was a cultural tendency to give more respect to someone who didn't need to write down their drafts. Writing was reserved for fully composed works; the person who actually wrote down notes during composition was seen as both absent minded and a bit wasteful. This was probably due in good measure to the time and trouble crafting paper or vellum required, but it also stemmed from the honor given to perfect memory and the respect shown in these days to the professional classes of fili, brehon, and clergy. To emulate them and appear professional and intelligent, most speakers spoke from memory and at the pitch that suited the assembly. Misjudging that volume, of course, got you a result that could be rather less than you had hoped. Cormac, who attended many gatherings and arbitrations of law in many sorts of settings, appears to be poking some sidelong fun at the shouters and mumblers he's seen as he advises his son.

Many of the lines in this particular counsel stress what we still see today as common courtesy: not shouting in conversation, not picking a fight, not being snide or trying to stir up trouble. It's impressive how common-sense many of these ancient thoughts on good civic discourse are to this day, and perhaps the words are a good reminder for modern people who sometimes assume that we're awfully sophisticated. A few words from our ancestors can remind us that good behavior, and bad behavior, are in some ways timeless.

### Abhcóide a Hocht
### Alt Fiche a Sé
### Tecosca Cormaic

'Cest, caté téchta flatha?' ol Carpre.
'Ní hansa,' ol Cormac.
rop sogcis,
rop sobraig,
rop saigthech,
rop soaccobrach,
rop soacallmach,
rop becda,

rop mórda,
rop dían,
rop fossaid,
rop fili,
rop fénech,
rop gáeth,
rop gartaid

rop sochraid,
rop sognais,
rop máeth,
rop crúaid,
rop carthach,

rop concardell,
rop fírén,
rop féig,
rop fedil,

rop ainmnetach,
rop áintech,
turgbad lubair la triunu,
bered fírbretha,
bíathad cach ndíllechta,

báthed cach n-anslicht,
miscniged gói,
carad fírinni,
rop dermatach uilc,
rop cuimnech mathiusa,

rop slúagach i ndálaib,
rop úathad i sanasaib,

rop sorche fri gnáis,
rop grían tige midchúarto,
rop airitid dála & airechta,

rop sercaid fis & érgnai,
rop cundrigid uilc,
rop smachtaid
coisc cáich mbes ingor,

míastar cách íarna thochus,
dobera a théchta do chách,

rop midid cáich iarna míad,
rop tairbertaid cáich
iarna ngrád & iarna ndán,

ropat dlúthe a nadmann,
ropat laxa a thobaig,
ropat áithe étrumma a
bretha & a chocerta,

'ar is triasna téchta sin
miditir ríg & flaithi,'
ol Cormac fri Carpre.

## Counsel the Eighth:
## Paragraph 6,
## The Counsels Of Cormac

"O Cormac, Grandson of Conn," said Cairbre,
"What are the qualities of a lord?"
"Not hard to tell," said Cormac
Let him honor geasa
Let him have self-mastery
Let him be a man of vigor
Let his desires be wholesome
Let him be of good will
Let him be affable
Let him be humble

Let him be quick
Let him be firm
Let him be a poet
Let him be wise
Let him know the laws

Let him be generous
Let him be genial
Let him be tender

Let him show that law must be obeyed
Let him show mercy

him be perceptive
Let him be constant
Let him be patient
Let him be moderate

Let him teach the strong to aid the weak,
Let him give justice
Let him feed every orphan

Let him quell the wrong
Let him despise the lie
Let him love the truth
Let him forget the foolish slight
Let him remember the kindness

Let him be attended by many in gatherings
Let him be attended by few in counsel

Let him shine in the company
Let him be the sun in the mead-hall
Let his hall be opened often to host the folk

Let him be a lover of knowledge
Let him be a scrounge of evils
Let him remind all of their duty

Let him give each person their due,
Let him be a judge of every soul
in the light of their place in life.

Let him pay liberal honors
to those of learning, skill and craft

Let his pledges be sure
Let his enforcement be lenient
Let his judgements be sharp and bright

For it is by those qualities
kings and lords are judged,"
said Cormac to Cairbre.

The literal translation for the line 'secure oaths assured' is 'the keeping of many hostages." This is uncomfortable to read for modern readers, so let's put it in cultural context. This was not a gun held to someone's head. In Old Ireland, the idea of hostage is less aggressive: "Hostages were used to make peace with enemies and/or to assert the submission of enemies; they were used to emphasize a ruler's internal political power; and they could be precursors to future relationships between the two parties," states the work 'The Cycles of the Kings'. According to this definition, a hostage would serve as 'collateral', as part of a contract, treaty, or as a guarantee for loyalty. Although it is clear how the modern definition derived from the older concept of 'hostage', the original definition is more political than anything else. Hostages would volunteer to be housed in the court of the party the oath was being made to, as sureties to make sure one's land would not be invaded:

"Lesser kings who did not have the power or allies to resist a hosting in their territory would often come to terms if the overking threatened to invade his territory or made a show of force at his border. Kings could reach an agreement at a meeting, and these could be guaranteed by the exchange of pledges or sureties." According to 'Early Irish Kingship and Succession'

In this situation, the hostages were essentially honored guests. They were not allowed to leave, but they were treated as part of the court and a valuable member of the lord's community... unless things went wrong, of course. There was always that.

For readers who know the stories of Niall of the Nine Hostages, this concept really helps us understand what his name means. It is not, 'Niall, the barbarian who's good at taking people against their will', but rather 'Niall, a king so great that he had assured bonds and hostage members of nine other great king's courts in his home.'

# Abhcóide a Naoi
# Alt a Naoi Déag
# Tecosca Cormaic

Rabhadh Cormac ad Carpre:
Ní bága fri ríg,
ní chomrís fri báeth,
ní chomthéis fri díbergach,
ní chomthana fri échtaid,

nír imthige fri roth
ná rout ná roilbe
ná romur
ná báegul
ná ga,
ní dlútha écnach,
ní ba thibre dála,
ní ba bronach cuirmthige,
ní ba dermatach dála,

ní ba dochoisc,
ní ba imresnaid fír,
ní ba aichneich for gói,
ní ba dochoisc,
ní ba imresnaid fír

ní ba aichneich for gói
ní ba foss foglaide,
ní ba chond ugra,

ní ba muine debtha,
ní ois do beólu do chách,
ní thairngire ná dotbé,

ní ba choibchech ar ná ba fíachach,
ní ba imgonaid ar ná ba mélachtnach,
ní ba chomramach ar ná ba miscnech,

ní ba imresnaid ar ná ba cennscoilte,
ní ba garg ar ná ba dobláith,
ní ba ugrach ar ná ba aitchennach,

ní ba éitir ar ná ba éslesach,
ní ba cotut ar ná ba dothcherna,

ní ba rogartaid ar ná ba aithbe,
ní ba lesc ar ná ba meirb,

ní ba roescaid ar ná ba dáiscuir,
ní ba debthach ar ná ba scarthach,

ní ba ráth ar neoch ar ná ba
eirse do chomaithech.

# Counsel The Ninth
## From Paragraph 18
## The Counsels Of Cormac

Warnings of King Cormac to Cairbre:
Don't threaten a king,
Don't consort with a fool,
Don't associate with a bully,
Don't consort with a criminal

Don't race a chariot on foot
Don't stand where a spear is aimed
Don't set yourself against the mountain,
Don't try to fight the tide,
Don't walk foolishly into peril

Don't join in slander,
Don't play the fool in the gathering,
Don't grumble in the alehouse
Don't forget your promises,
Don't be argumentative,
Don't quarrel with the truth

Don't be a clever liar,
Don't aid a thief,
Don't start the argument

Don't be a thicket of strife,
Don't make a promise to a great many folk,
Don't promise what you don't have

Don't be a spendthrift, and you'll avoid debt
Don't be aggressive, and you'll avoid disgrace
Don't be argumentative, and you'll
avoid animosity

Don't be quarrelsome, and you won't
get your head broken
Don't be rough, and you won't be a lout
Don't be combative, and you won't
get your nose bloodied

Don't be absent, lest you be negligent
Don't be brusque, lest you be rude

Don't feed others so well that you become thin,
Don't be lazy, lest that you lose your vigor,

Don't be over-eager,
lest you make a fool of yourself
Don't be contentious,
lest others cease to invite you in

Don't guarantee
what you can't provide
to your neighbors

**A** word on original translation: in the original manuscript, seven types of fool who should not be dealt with are named in the second stanza of this counsel. Kuno Meyer translated it in this manner:

> ní cria di secht mbáethaib file la Féne,
> .i. di mnái, di chimbid, di mesc,
> di drúth, di dásachtach, di ardd,
> di arusc

> do not buy from the seven fools according to the law of the Irish,
> viz. from a house woman, from a caitiff (?), from a drunken person,
> from a buffoon, from a madman, from a ? from a ?, from a ?

Since this section was so badly damaged that more than half of it is illegible, the later translator Thomas Cleary glossed it as 'the six unqualified persons'. He names these persons as a housewife, a drunk, a moron, a madman, a noble, and a blind person. But his is the only source that renders the list in this way.

'Unqualified persons' is definitely a better translation of mbáethaib than 'fools'. But I prefer to avoid the venal sin Meyer ever so often commited of guessing about some words (though, to give him credit, he always marked these words with either an ellipse or a question mark.)

Given that no two sources could agree on the translation of this passage, and the original manuscript is at this point unreadable in this area, I've decided to leave this contested passage out altogether in the illustration. Better not to speak than to tell a lie, so they say.

### Abhcóide a Deich
### Alt a Hocht
### Tecosca Cormaic

'A húi Chuind, a Chormaic,' ol Carpre,
'cia bátar do gníma intan ropsa gilla?'
'Ní hansa,' ol Cormac.

'Nogonainn muic, nolenainn lorc i mba m'óenur,
nocinginn ar chuire cóicir i mba cóicer,
ba-sa oirgnech imbsa dechenborach,
ba-sa indredach imbsa fichtech,
ba-sa cathach imbsa cétach —
rop íat sin mo gníma,' ol Cormac fri Carpre.

### Counsel the Tenth
### From Paragraph 8
### Tecosca Cormaic

"O Cormac, grandson of Conn," said Cairbre, "what were your deeds when you were a young man?"
"Not hard to tell," said Cormac,

"I would kill a boar and follow a track when I was alone,
I would march against a band of five when I was in a band of five,
I was ready to kill when I was in a band of ten,
I was ready to raid when I was in a band of twenty,
I was ready to give battle when I was in a band of a hundred
these were my deeds," said Cormac to Cairbre.

Though this is one of the shorter Counsels, it contains a wealth of detail about Irish culture. In this counsel, Cormac is advising his son on several things at once: both how to use common sense when making tactical decisions, and what activities are worth engaging in. This is where the words open a door for us into the Old Irish world.

Today, cattle are big business in Ireland. As of 2012, there were 139,000 farms in Ireland, 110,000 farming 6.6 million cattle. In ancient Ireland, cattle were more than just cash: they were pride, and they were prosperity incarnate. In pre-Christian days, a person's wealth was measured not in currency or in land—given that land was held communally by each tribe, this makes very good sense—but in the number of cattle one owned. If you wanted more prestige, you could breed more cattle, barter more cattle...or steal them.

Cattle raiding was a way of life to the early Irish people. It was seen as sport, an opportunity to show off one's skill, acquire wealth, and shame one's enemies. Scholars suggest that at any given period between 400 and 1100 CE there were between 100–150 tribes in Ireland, so there were plenty of neighbors to play the game with. Most tribes were made up of a handful of kin-groups (fine) numbering about 3,000 men, women and children. All together, they'd be described as a tuath, which translates directly as 'people' or loosely as 'tribe' in English. At the head of each tribe was a King (rí) and, though most kings oversaw their own tribe alone, some were voted in or claimed power in battle to become Over-Kings (ruire) or Provincial Kings (rí ruireach). The Provincial Kings attended council and paid tribute to the High King (ard rí) who arbitrated between them.

Interestingly, a number of sources stress that kings could not make law; that was the work of the brehon. This early separation of branches of power was one of the pillars of Irish society, ensuring that no one leader began to act despotically.

But all that was very far away for your average small rí. He was interested in seeing that his community was cared for, entertained, and that young people didn't get restless. Raids were the perfect answer to this. A newly appointed king was expected to lead his men in a raid following his inauguration as a part of the celebration; in fact, there are some records showing that communities set aside cattle to be ritually rustled by the new king. And because this was the norm, it wasn't wise for young men to leave the territories of their tuath and their communities; it was inviting the claim that you were out raiding, and a good thrashing by lads from other towns. Better to either go in groups, or not at all, until you were a trained professional who was recognized as traveling on the legitimate errands of your craft everywhere in the country.

With that understanding, we can read this counsel much more clearly: Cormac is telling his son 'boy, when I was your age I'd go hunting alone, but I wasn't so wild that I'd leave town without my friends with me, and a good lot of us if we were planning to start anything. That's what I did when I was a lad. Use your head and do the same.'

**Abhcóide a Haon Déag**
**Alt Tríocha Dó**
**Tecosca Cormaic**

'A húi Chuind, a Chormaic,' ol Carpre,
'cate forus cuitbeda la Féine?' 'Ni hansa,' ol Cormac.

Fer sotal im gáis, im dán, im thocad,
fer suirig míadach máithmech,
5] fer lesc lond timm teichmech,
fer báeth borb brasbríathrach,
fer fergach forránach forsmachtach,
fer neóit anfossaid étaid
'coirpetae ecal ocal opunn anfaitech
ansercach anraitech imda andíarraid.'

## Counsel the Eleventh
## From Paragraph 32
## The Counsels Of Cormac

"O grandson of Conn, Cormac," said Cairbre,
"what is the basis of ridicule among the Irish?"
"Not hard to tell," said Cormac
A man arrogant in his wisdom, his gifts, or his good fortune,
A man who is foppish, prideful, vainglorious
A man who is lazy, irascible, distractible
A man who is thoughtless, foolish, boastful
A man who is violent, argumentative, overbearing
A man who is stingy, unreliable, jealous
A man who is corrupt, stingy, easily offended
A man who is hasty, uncaring, tactless
A man who is churlish, senseless, demanding."

In illustrating this counsel, I've chosen to again showcase the Irish connection between rats in the granary and secretive crimes. The central figure, a rather naughty monk drinking more than he should of the local wine, is drawn from an illustration in the thirteenth-century manuscript 'Li livres dou santé' by Aldobrandino of Siena. Though the inspiration is slightly modern for the material, the image was so perfect for encapsulating the qualities that are being censored that I couldn't pass it up.

In the illustration, we see a monk, a theoretically holy figure, who has been entrusted with keys representing responsibilities and privileges. But in spite of his vows and the trust that has been put in him, he has chosen to do as he pleases and indulge his appetites.
When a figure of authority acts in this manner, Cormac clearly felt he deserved a piece of satire like this counsel being spoken against him.

# Abhcóide a Dó Dhéag
## Alt a Dó Dhéag
### Tecosca Cormaic

'A húi Chuind, a Chormaic,' ol Carpre,
cid as fó dam?'
'Ní hansa,' ol Cormac.
'Ma contúaissi frim thecosc,

ní cuitbe nach sen ciarba óc,

ná bocht ciarba soimm,

ná nocht ciarba suim,

ná losc ciarba lúath,

ná dall ciarba féig,

ná lobor ciarba thrén,

ná borb ciarba threbar,

ná óinmit ciarba gáeth,

nírba lesc,

nírba lonn,

nírba súanach,

nírba neóit,

nírba deáith,

nírba étaid,

ar cach lesc lond súanach
neóit deáith étaid is miscais Dé & dóine.'

# Counsel The Twelfth
# From Paragraph 12
# The Counsels Of Cormac

"O Cormac, grandson of Conn," said Cairbre,
"what is best for me?"
"Not hard to tell," said Cormac,
"This is what I have to teach,"

do not scorn the elderly, though you be young,

nor the poor, though you be rich,

nor the naked, though you be finely-dressed

nor the lame, though you be fleet,

nor the blind, though you be keen of sight,

nor the weak, though you be strong,

nor the dull, though you be clever,

nor the fool, though you be wise.

Be not sluggish,

be not irascible,

be not slothful,

be not stingy,

be not idle,

be not jealous.

for the sluggish, the irascible, the slothful,
the stingy, the idle and the jealous,
and before them all the one who scorns;
these are hateful before God and society."

    One of the things I love about this work is that, under the formal language, the lessons are so very human. Cairbre is Cormac's son, so in this work a boy is sitting down with his father, asking the age-old question: 'hey dad? How do I do the right thing?'

    And the father answers 'well son, let me tell you. You don't pick on people who can't keep up with you, you don't lay around, you help people out and you don't get nasty. If you're laying around, you're stingy, if you're mean, nobody's going to have much time for you. But if you walk around laughing at everybody and picking on them, oh then you'll really have no friends. That's about it.'

### Abhcóidea Trí Déag
### Alt a Fiche Aon
### Tecosca Cormaic

'A húi Chuind, a Chormaic,' ol Carpre,
'cid as messam do chorp duine?'
'Ní hansa,' ar Cormac.
'Rosuide,
rolige,
airissem fota,
tócbála tromma,
fedmanna ós niurt,
élud elta,
roretha,
roléimenna,
tuitmenna mince,
coss tar crann siúil,
éirimm grib,
silliud fri grís,
dallchéimmenna,
cér,
nús,
núa corma,
tarb,
táth,
turach,
uisce móna,
mochéirge,
úacht,
grían,
gorta,
roól,
rosáith,
rochotlud,
ropheccad,
cuma,
rith fri hard,
gairm fri gáith,
beimm ós niurt,
tirad,
samdrúcht,
gamdrúcht,
slige luaithred,
snám iar sáith,
cotlud fóen,
deoch mór,
baile, báithe.'

## Counsel The Thirteenth
## From Paragraph 21
## The Counsels Of Cormac

"O Cormac, grandson of Conn," said Cairbre,
"What is worst for the human body?"
'Not hard to tell," said Cormac
"Sitting too long,
lying too long,
being inactive,

heavy lifting,
Overexertion,
Loneliness

Too much running,
Too much leaping,
Too much clumsiness

Sleeping with a leg over the bed rail,
Seating a fast horse too often,
Staring at fire,
Walking in the dark,
Hot wax,
Beestings,
new ale,
Bull-flesh,
Curdled milk,
dry food,

bog-water,
rising too early,
cold,
Sun,
hunger

Drinking much,
eating much,
Sleeping much,
sinning much,

Melancholy,
running uphill,
shouting into the wind,
a blow beyond one's strength,

drying oneself by a fire,
summer-dew,
Winter-dew,
beating ashes,

swimming with a full belly,
Lying flat to sleep,
Gulping the drink,
frenzy,
Foolhardiness."

This fascinating list of unhealthy habits shows us both what was socially acceptable to the Irish people in Cormac's time, and what resources and dangers existed in their world. Some of the unhealthy behaviors are quite common-sense—gulping the drink or getting too much sun, for instance—but some of them strike a modern reader as rather odd. For instance, why was bull flesh seen as bad for you? Why not dry yourself by the fire? What's wrong with riding a horse for a while? Or beating ashes and sleeping with a leg over the bed rail?

Let's discuss these a bit and give the points some context.

Bull flesh—that is, meat from the carcass of a bull, particularly one who has lived past his first few years—is lean, without a lot of the fat that creates marbling. Flavor from beef has a lot to do with marbling, the most richly flavored being the best-marbled. In addition, in a situation of damp cold without central heating, the human body craves calories and fats. This predilection stayed true well into the Victorian Era, and was remarked on specifically in the work of Ruth Goodman, an experimental archeologist who goes out and lives historically accurate routines as closely as possible in order to comment on the effects and effectiveness of various practices from personal experience. She's written several fascinating books, and in 'How To Be A Victorian', she writes 'living in a barely heated Victoran house through a whole winter and engaging in the daily physical routine of Victorian domestic and farming lifestyle, I found that my appetite and tastes temporarily changed. Foods that I would simply dismiss in my twenty-first century life became delicious... my body was telling me in no uncertain terms that it needed plenty of carbohydrates and animal fats to sustain the lifestyle."

A 9th century Irish home was not much warmer than a Victorian home (though the inhabitants did have the benefit of avoiding the breathing of coal smoke.) In this context, and indeed in recorded information that comes down from this time, the flesh from an older bull was sold as a poor cut of meat, one you'd pass up if you could. In the modern world, such animals usually end up in ground chuck, where the meat's shortcomings aren't as noticeable. In Cormac's time and place, this sort of meat was fed to dogs and those who couldn't afford better.

Speaking of fires, 'beating the ashes' wasn't a healthy chore. It was done by the lowest class of people, usually bondsmen (those who'd gotten so far into debt that they were required to do menial work for their debtors in order to pay it off) and consisted of beating ashes out of a well-to-do person's rushes and (among the wealthy) rugs. It was used as an idiom used for anything involving cleaning ashes. When this work was done, tiny bits of particulate were breathed in, damaging lung tissue. It really wasn't good for you.

It was also believed that the change of temperature that arose between sitting huddled up next to the fire and walking about the rest of the house was unhealthy. When someone came in cold and wet, it was recommended that they be warmed up with blankets and heated ale or (if available) wine rather than being seated by the hot fire in works like the 'Regimen Sanitatis' and the work now called 'Three Irish Medical Glossaries'.

Now, about seating a horse. Few of us in the 21st century have done a lot of riding, but those who have know what this is about. Writing for 'Horse Nation', Kristen Kovach tells us:
"From bouncing beginners to trail bosses to equestrian triathletes, we all know saddle sore is a teacake term for various uncomfortable ailments one can contract by riding a horse. Described in very genteel terms, sores can occur on the buttocks from, well, any number of things. It can occur on those little seat bones between one's legs (ischia). It can occur on one's "Mr. or Ms. Happy."

The most bizarre and unnerving saddle sore I've endured was crotch mumps. Crotch mumps feel as though tennis balls have been duct taped to your inner thighs. It feels worse than it looks. Mostly it's sore, like a bruise combined with the sensation of stuffing two dish towels in your undies and trying to walk."

And how about 'dry food', why would that be seen as unhealthy?
In Middle Irish, the words for 'food' and 'bread' were often interchangeable. Dry bread, without butter, cheese, or any sort of spread, was both fairly low in nutritional value and—let's face it—not particularly pleasant to eat.

Then there's the commentary on social issues. Take the notes on overeating and lazing about: these still resonate with us today. How about loneliness? Though we understand it intuitively as unpleasant, modern research has shown us that loneliness is literally unhealthy.
The CDC has written:

-Social isolation significantly increased a person's risk of premature death from all causes, a risk that may rival those of smoking, obesity, and physical inactivity.

-Social isolation was associated with about a 50% percent increased risk of dementia.

-Loneliness among heart failure patients was associated with a nearly 4 times increased risk of death, 68% increased risk of hospitalization, and 57% increased risk of emergency department visits.
-Poor social relationships (characterized by social isolation or loneliness) was associated with a 29% increased risk of heart disease and a 32% increased risk of stroke.

-Loneliness was associated with higher rates of depression, anxiety, and suicide.

What we've now researched and proved scientifically, Cormac observed and recorded empirically.

But how about sleeping with your leg over the bed rail? This, again, is Cormac's sly and humorous social commentary cropping up. 'A leg over the bed rail' was a Middle Irish idiom for what we now call 'getting a leg over', with the particular insinuation that someone might be in a bed that isn't theirs. In the context of its time, this line would have provided a dirty little chuckle and helped the whole list stick in the mind. Some things really do not change.

**Abhcóide a Ceathair Déag**
**Alt a Haon Déag**
**Tecosca Cormaic**

'A húi Chuind, a Chormaic,' ol Carpre,
'cid as dech dam?'
'Ní hansa,' ol Cormac.
'Ma contúaisi frim thecosc,
nír tharta th'enech ar choirm ná ar biad,
ar is ferr dín cloth oldás dín mbiid.'

Nírba úallach minba trebthach,
nírba sriangabrach cen eocho,
nírba ólchobrach cen choirm,
nírba lachtmar cen bú,
nírba massech mani bet cáerchach,

ar is col i ndálaib
in domain úall cen trebad,
téte cen eochu,
ólchobra cen choirm,
lachtmaire cen bú,
maisse cen cáircha.'

Counsel The Fourteenth
From Paragraph 11
The Counsels Of Cormac

"O Cormac, grandson of Conn," said Cairbre,
"What is best for me?"
"Not hard to tell," said Cormac.
If you heed my advice,
you will not trade your honor for ale or food.
It is better to save one's good name than to save one's food
Don't be proud unless you are a land-owner
Don't keep mares without stallions
Don't give feasts without first brewing ale
Be sparing with the milk
unless you have cattle
Don't dress finely
if you have no sheep
For pride without production,
luxury without husbandry,
entertainment without work,
drinking the milk without raising the cow,
fine dress without feeding the sheep,
These things are a crime
against the folk of the world."

## Abhcóide a Cúig Déag
## Alt a Ceathair Déag
## Tecosca Cormaic

'A húi Chuind, a Chormaic,' ol Carpre,
'ocus gabála báise cis lir?'
'Ní hansa,' ol Cormac.

Luge ria mbreith,
bretha díana,
dúscud ferge,

folabra gúach,
cairigud fír,
freitech derthige,

tintúd breth,
brón oc fleid,
flaithem gúach,

gáire im sen,
senchas do chleith,
cluiche for aill,

erchor cen chommus,
comrith fri báeth,
mórthu fri ríg,

recht cen chomallad,
comallad cech uilc,
olc fri carddinc,

cétlud fri cách,
gel cech núa,
náma cech gnáth,

gním cen fiadnaisi,
fíada tláith,
turfochraic breth,

bith cen seotu,
airlicud il,
ilar carat,

brón fri ríg,
rolabra cen gáis, —

'is í sin gabáil báise,' ar Cormac.

Counsel The Fifteenth
From Paragraph 14
The Counsels Of Cormac

"O Cormac, grandson of Conn," said Cairbre,
"the ways of folly, what is their number?'
'Not hard to tell,' said Cormac.

Swearing after a legal ruling,
Hasty decisions,
Rousing anger,

Lying whispers,
Cruel truths,
A failure of piety

Recanting a judgment given,
Sour words at a feast,
Lying words from the mouth of a chief

Mocking the elders,
Misrepresenting history,
Dancing on a cliff

Shooting without a target,
Competing with those
who cannot stand against you,
Haughtiness with those
who are owed respect

Failure to honor the law,
Performance of wrongs,
Doing disservice to friends

Betrayal to lovers,
Enchantment with passing novelties,
Contempt for the traditional

Action without evidence,
Incompetence in one's responsibilities,
Paying to sway legal decisions

Wasting what is gained,
Lending too much,
Counting friends by number
rather than value

Grumbling and groaning at the King,
Much talk with little reason,

"These are the ways of folly," said Cormac.

What is particularly interesting about this counsel is that, in amongst the remarks on basic civility—disservice to friends, griping to the King, and so forth—the deep importance and respect for the Brehon Law is repeatedly mentioned. In this culture, the Brehon law was seen as a mutually agreed-upon and absolutely legitimate system of adjudication between members of a community, with deep historical precedent as well as contemporary approval supporting it. To disrespect the law was to disrespect the legitimacy of the entire community.

The Old Irish word for piety, crábud, can also be read as 'loyalty' or 'devotion', and we can understand this as religious piety, but also as loyalty to the good order of the community itself. Swearing after a legal ruling, given this context, wasn't simply boorish: it was a slander to the laws held in respect by the majority of the community. To misrepresent history was to damage the fabric of law and tradition that supported society, and it was much more harmful in a time when much of the legitimacy of a practice was based in its historical antecedents. And acting without evidence—that is, without a legally justifiable cause for the act—brought shame and possible fines down upon the actor and those tied to them by familial or communal ties. Interestingly, it could also come down on the Brehon who gives a judgment without cause.

In the Brehon system, each Brehon was assigned a rank by the levels of study and the numbers of examinations they had fulfilled. When one Brehon had given judgment on a case, a plaintiff could offer a security—collateral of some kind that would belong to the defendant if the case went against them—and appeal to a Brehon of a higher rank. The grounds of appeal most frequently noticed are "sudden judgments," meaning judgements given without sufficient consideration or bias on the part of the judge. If it was found that the lower Brehon had given an illegal, unfair, or personally motivated ruling, they had to supply a fine of the same worth as the collateral that the plaintiff put up. Through this system, Brehon were very personally incentivized to give sensible, well considered, and impartial judgements. This ensured the legitimacy of the entire legal system, since the community understood implicitly that giving poor rulings would cost the Brehon themselves dearly.

**Abhcóide a Sé Déag**
**Alt a Naoí agus Deich**
**Tecosca Cormaic**

'A húi Chuind, a Chormaic,' ol Carpre,
'cid messam lat adchondarc?'
'Ní hansa,' ol Cormac.

An rud is measa atá feicthe agam?
Gnúsi námat
i rói chatha.

Agus an rud is fearr atá feicthe agam?
Ilach íar mbúaid,
molad íar lúag,
itge degmná dia hadurt.

**Counsel The Sixteenth**
**From Paragraph 9&10**
**The Counsels Of Cormac**

"Cormac, grandson of Conn," said Cairbre,
"what do you deem the best and worst things you have seen?"
"Not hard to tell," said Cormac.
"The worst thing I have seen?
Faces of the enemy
Arrayed against me
On the field of war

Now, the best thing I have seen?
A gathering in song after victory
Praises given with just reward
A lady's invitation to adore her.

In this entry, two very short counsels have been combined into a coherent whole. What a society sees as best and worst in the world tells us a great deal about what is valued. And much of what was valued in early Ireland was just desert for each act, and victory after battle.

In the days of Cormac's father Art, and somewhat in his day as well, warfare was a fact of life. Politically, Ireland was organized into independent tuatha (clans) under their elected king.

Surrounding a king was the airi aicme (the upper class), whose land and property rights were clearly defined in the Brehon Law. Below them were each of the ranks of artisans, craftsmen, freemen and bondsmen. As a general rule, the system worked well, but there was a regular conflict between neighboring tuatha. It could be as small as a cattle raid, which was the local football game of its time, or as large as an armed attempt to claim the neighboring property and goods.

These inter-tuatha conflicts steadily became less common as high kings began to be elected and took on the work of mediating between the ri of each area, but in Cormac's days the unpleasantness of facing enemies on the field—especially when you were slightly outnumbered—would be familiar to all contemporary listeners. The sweetness of victory would be equally familiar, and very much relished.

And the joy of being invited by a lady? That, of course, is timeless.

### Abhcóide a Seacht Déag
### Alt a Trí Déag
### Tecosca Cormaic

'A húi Chuind, a Chormaic,' ol Carpre,
'cia étargen síl nÁdaim?'
'Ní hansa,' ol Cormac. 'Nosnetargén uili, fir, mná, maic
sceo ingena archena.'
'Cinnas ón?' ol Carpre.
Gáeth cach fossaid,
fírén cech fíal,
fedil cech ainmnetach,
fissid cech foglaintid,
10] fúarrech cech finechar,

fáilid cech slán,
suánach cech slemon,
serb cech borb,

báeth cech trén,
tibir cech mer,
múcna cech mog,

mórda cech ndindba,
imresnaid cech n-aneólach,
anbal cech anecnaid,
ecal cech uamnach,
inraicc cech lobur,
altromaid cech dochraid,

ál cech angtha,
faitech cech uaimnech,
andgid cech ecal

diupartach cech ndindba,
dálach cech cosnamach,
conchar cech sáithech,

solepthach cech suirgech,
sétach cech selbach,
slichtlethan cech sáer,

sothcherna cech suaibsech
menmar cach cáinte,
solam cech marcach,

domblas cech gó,
milis cech fír,

milbéla druinecha,
dálacha drochmná,
dodáil a maic, mairg oca mbíat!

**Counsel The Seventeenth**
**From Paragraph 13**
**The Counsels Of Cormac**

"O Cormac, grandson of Conn," said Cairbre,
"What distinguishes the people of our race?"
"Not hard to tell," said Cormac.

"I distinguish them all,
both men, women, sons and daughters."
"How is that?" Cairbre asked.

Cormac said:
One who is steadfast is wise,
One who is generous is blessed,
One who is patient will persevere

One who is studious learns much,
One who loves the family is gentle,
One who is healthy is cheerful

One who is rash is a laughing stock,
One who is in bondage is gloomy,
One who is poor is proud

One who is ignorant is quarrelsome,
One who is unwise is shameless,
One who is timid fears much

One who knows illness is honest,
One who knows suffering is compassionate,
One who carries anxieties is afflicted

One who is haunted by fear is cautious
One who is pleased by fear is cruel
One who is starving will steal

One who is contentious is often in court
One who is full of life
loves the belling of the hounds on the hunt
One who is full of love
spends much time in the marital bed

A landlord is rich,
A craftsman is versatile,
A good man is generous

A satirist is dangerous,
A horseman is nimble,
A lie is bitter, a truth is sweet

The skillful woman is sweet-tongued
The ill-favored woman is venomous
Ill-met are her sons, a sorrow to him who meets them!

### Abhcóide a Hocht Déag
### Alt a Cúig Déag
### Tecosca Cormaic

Dligid ecna airmitin,
arfich gáis gail,
tomtenach cech n-uamnach,

torsech cech sercach,
crimnach cech galrach,
imresnach cech gúach,

gáibthech cech báeth,
báeglach cech labor,
imgonaid cech lond,

trebar cech trebthach,
dreman cech drochláech,
anbal cech rudrach,

úathmar cech ecal,
adúathmar cech ndorcha,
ísel cech athech,

collach cech sámach,
díscir cech dona,
uamnach cech cintach,
fán cech aithisech,

ecal cech faittech,
cosáitech cech dotheng,
án cech cétludach,

dálach cech dagthúath,
dúnadach cech degrí,
sétrech cech saigthech,

suabais cach dána,
éslessach cech brass,
gúach cech tairngertach,

soisil cech bronntach,
cuitbide cech denmnetach,
athissech cech coimsech,
arrachtach cech athissech,
coimsech cech céillid,

comairlech cech irisech,
midlaech cech díchoisc,
sái cech sochoisc,
aititiu cech indraic,
innmusach cech dán maith,
dóinech cech dindba

## Counsel The Eighteenth
## From Paragraph 15
## The Counsels Of Cormac

Knowledge deserves to be honored,
wisdom vanquishes strength,
The skeptical give many opinions

One who loves is sorrowful
One who suffers is cantankerous,
One who deceives will be suspicious

A fool is dangerous
A blowhard is in peril,
A fighter is ready to brawl

A good farmer is full of prudence,
A bad warrior is full of fury,
A covetous man is empty of shame

A danger is dreadful
A darkness is fearful
A rent-bonded one hangs their head low

An idler is corpulent,
A desperate man is shameless,
A guilty man is apprehensive,

A mocking man is loud-voiced
A cautious man is quiet-voiced
An evil mind has a quarrelsome tongue

The cheerful man is fond of gatherings,
The good clan is fond of assembling,
The good king is fond of hosting

The litigious one grumbles,
The courageous one is gentle,
The violent one is remiss in their duties

One who tells the future is lying
One who wastes is a fool
One who is impatient is ridiculous

One who has power is in risk of being reviled,
One who shouts insults is a coward,
One who is well-disciplined is wise

One who is sensible is competent
One who is honest acknowledges rights
One who has known suffering is humane.

**Abhcóide a Naoí Déag**
**Alt a Ceathair**
**Tecosca Cormaic**

'A húi Chuind, a Chormaic,'
ol Carpre, 'cadeat ada flatha & cuirmthige?'
'Ní hansa,' ol Cormac.
Costud im dagflaith,
Lassamna do lochrannaib,
Luthbas im [dot ]sochaide,

Samugud suide,
Soichlige do dáleman,
Díanlám oc fodail,
Fochraibe oc timthirecht,

Tigerna do charthain,
Mesrugud senma,
Scélugud ngairit,
Gnúis fáilid,

Fáilte fri dáma,
Tóe fri comad,
Cocetla bindi,

'it é sin adae flatha & cormthige,'
ol Cormac fri Carpre.

## Counsel the Nineteenth
## From Paragraph 4
## The Counsels Of Cormac

"O Cormac, Grandson of Conn," said Cairbre,
"what is fitting for both a chieftain's hall and an ale house?"
"Not hard to tell," said Cormac,

"Affability in the company of worthy folk,
A well-lit place of many lanterns,
Good effort made to bring joy to the gathering,

A seat for every soul
A generous hand in giving,
A nimble hand in filling the bowls,
Readiness of supply

Loyalty and respect,
Pleasure balanced with good sense,
A story with no boast in it

A cheerful face,
Welcoming the poets,
Silence during the recitation of wisdom,
Strong voice in song with your fellows.

These things make both an ale-house
and a chieftain's hall good," said Cormac.

**Abhcóide a Fiche**
**Alt a Cúig**
**Tecosca Cormaic**

'A húi Chuind, a Chormaic,'
ol Carpre, 'cid asa ngaibther
flaithemnas for túathaib
& chlandaib & chenćaib?'
'Ní hansa,' ol Cormac.

'A feib chrotha

cheneóil & érgnai,

a gáis

ordan

eslabrai

inraccus,

a feib dúthchusa airlabra,

a nirt imgona sochraite gaibther.'

### Counsel The Twentieth
### From Paragraph 5
### The Counsels Of Cormac

"Oh Cormac, grandson of Conn,"
said Cairbre, "how does a chieftain show
that he is worthy of his station?"
"Not hard to tell," said Cormac,

It is gained by excellence:

Excellence of appearance

Excellence of gathering

Excellence of discernment

Excellence of family

Excellence of integrity

Excellence of eloquence

It is shown by the absence of outlaws,
It is shown by the presence of many friends."

## Abhcóide a Fiche Haon
## Alt a Fiche Seacht agus a Fiche Hocht
## Tecosca Cormaic

'A húi Chuind, a Chormaic,' ol Carpre,
'cia mesam frismbia condelg duit?' '
Ní hansa,' ol Cormac.

Fer co n-ainbli cáinti,
co n-ugra cumaile,
co foilli con cermna,
co cubus con,
col-láim latrainn,
co nirt tairb,
10] co n-érgna bretheman,
co n-ecna airctech amnus,

co n-erlabra fir sochraid,
co cuimne senchada,
co n-airbert comarba,
co luga echthadat,
'os é gáeth gúach líath lond lugach
labar a n-asbeir 'tairnic, tung, tithis."

Fer garb
serb borb
lonn dían

dóescair díscir
dermatach engach
anbal iarngáesach

nád ana nech fris,
níana fri nech.

Ní bind lais-sium a n-asbeir nech,

ní bind la nech a n-asbeir sium,

is e co n-urgairt túaithe & eclaise.'

## Counsel the Twenty First
## From Paragraph 27&28
## The Counsels Of Cormac

"O Cormac, Grandson of Conn," said Cairbre,
"What are the unworthy qualities
which you compare with these?"
"That's easy," said Cormac

"The shamelessness of a satirist,
With the memory of a historian

The integrity of a wretch,
Paired to the cunning of a cur,

The conscience of a dog,
with the hand of a thief,

The strength of a bull,
With the contentiousness of a lawyer,

The craftiness of a weasel,
With the speech of a wealthy man,

The habits of an heir,
With the oath of a horse thief

Shrewdness, deceit, hoarfrost-coldness,
vehemence, a tongue for cursing.
And above all, an arrogant speech:
"It is settled! I swear it! I'll take an oath on it!"

The rough,
The bitter,
The rude,

The violent,
The vehement,
The vulgar,

The impetuous,
The forgetful,
The noisy,

The audacious,
Wise after the fact,

He waits for no one,
and who no one waits for,
He does not heed
and is not heeded,
He is shunned
by the folk and the faith."

Abhcóide a Fiche Dó
Alt a Tríocha Cúig agus a Seacht Déag
Tecosca Cormaic

'A húi Chuind,
cid buidre lat rochúala?'
'Ní hansa.'
Trú cusa mberar robad,
nech ara condegar ní nád cara,
risi mná báithe.
Máthair etha aig,
athair saille snechta,
túar fola fleochud,
túar tedma tart,
andsom gobél gáeth,
dech do shínaib ceó,
ferr a bráthair bróen,
acht do muir ní thor
thech torann.

## Counsel The Twenty-Second
## From Paragraph 35&17
## The Counsels Of Cormac

"Oh Cormac, grandson of Conn,"
said Cairbre, "What is best for the seasons?"
"Easy enough,
Winter fine and frosty,
Spring dry and breezy,
Summer dry and showery,
Autumn dewy and fruitful."
"And how do you read the weathers?"
"Not hard to tell," said Cormac,
"Ice is mother to grain
Snow is father to bacon
Wet is forewarning of feud
Drought is promise of plague
Wind is troublesome in the straits,
the best of weathers is mist,
better his brother rain,
Thunder has no value,
Lest it be the thunder of the sea."

**Abhcóide a Fíche Trí**
**Alt a Fíche Naoi**
**Tecosca Cormaic**

'A húi Chuind, a Chormaic,' ol Carpre,
'is áil dam-sa co fessur cindas
beo itir gáethu & báethu,
itir gnáthu & ingnathu, itir senu & ócu,
itir engu & anengu.' '
Ní hansa,' ol Cormac.

Ní ba rogáeth, ní ba robáeth,
ní ba roúallach, ní ba dimbrígach,
ní ba romórda, ní ba robecda,
ní ba rolabar, ní ba rothó,
ní ba rochrúaid, ní ba rothimm,
Dia mba rogáeth, fritotsáilfider,
dia mba robáeth, nottogáethfaider,
dia mba roúallach, notdimdaigfaider,
dia mba robecda, bid dígráid,

dia mba rolabar, bid dérgna,
dia mba rothó, nitsúilfider,
dia mba rochrúaid, fordotbrisfider,
dia mba rothimm, notdreisfider.

## Counsel The Twenty-Third
## From Paragraph 29
## The Counsels Of Cormac

"O grandson of Conn," said Cairbre,
"I wish to know how I shall behave
among the wise and the foolish,
among friends and strangers,
among the old and the young,
among the innocent and the wicked."
"Not hard to tell," said Cormac.
"Be not too wise, be not too foolish,
be not too conceited, be not too timid,
be not too haughty, be not too humble,
be not too talkative, be not too silent,
be not too harsh, be not too feeble
Too wise, and expectations will be imposed on you
Too foolish, and you'll be duped
Too conceited, and you'll be devoid of friendship
Too timid, and you'll be robbed of dignity

Too talkative, and you'll be dismissed
Too silent, and you'll be disregarded
Too hard, and you'll be broken,
Too soft, and you'll be squashed."

**P**aragraph 29 of the Counsel, which starts with Cairbre's question about how he should behave, seems to have been written as an echo of Paragraph 7. In fact, many of the adjectives are mirrored almost exactly.

| Paragraph 29 | Paragraph 7 |
| --- | --- |
| nipsa rochrúaid | nipsa roirusa |
| nipsa rothim | ni ba rothimm |

Both passages warn a young man against being too harsh (rochrúaid), but also against being too meek (rothim), although they prescribe only having enough wits (basa gaeth, 'be wise'), and not too many (ni ba rogáeth, 'be not too wise'). Many of the ideas are also echoed, but where they're in their positive form in Paragraph 7, they're reframed as warnings in Paragraph 29.

From Paragraph 7
ba tó fásaig, ba labor sochuide
'I was quiet in the wilderness; I was talkative in a crowd'

From Paragraph 29
ní ba rolabar, ní ba rothó,
'Be not too talkative, be not too silent'

It's important to stress the contrast between the passages here: while Paragraph 7 instructs Cairbre (and all youngsters) to behave appropriately for given situations, Paragraph 29 reframes each situation as a warning against acting outside of moderate parameters.

It's quite possible that Paragraph 29 was inspired by Paragraph 7, created as a companion piece to both reinforce and bookend it.

## Abhcóide a Ceathair
## Alt a Tríocha
## Tecosca Cormaic

'Cest,' ol Carpre, 'cindas nombeo?'
'Ní hansa,' ol Cormac.

Ba gáeth fri gáis ar ná rottogáitha nech i ngáis,

ba úallach fri úaill ar ná tucca nech crith fort,

ba becda fri becdataid a ndéntar do thol,

ba labar fri labra …

ba tó fri tói i n-éitsider aisnéis,

ba crúaid fri crúas ar náchattarda nech i n-éislis,

ba móeth fri móithi ar náchatrochru cách.

## Counsel The Twenty-Fourth
## From Paragraph 30
## Tecosca Cormaic

"A question, my father," said Cairbre, "how should I be?"
"That's easy," said Cormac

Be knowledgeable to the learned,
So that you will not be duped

Be proud to the haughty,
So that you will not be made to quail

Be humble to the humble,
And your will shall be theirs

Be talkative with the talking,
So that you will be heard

Be silent with the quiet
So that you will be able to hear

Be hard with the harsh,
So that you will not be humiliated

Be soft with the soft
And bring no unkindness down upon you."

### Abhcóide a Fiche Cúig
### Alt a Tríocha Ceathair
### Tecosca Cormaic

'A maic, ma contúaisi frim,' ol Cormac,
'is é mo chosc duit:'

Ní bad rechtaire duit fer co célib,

ní bad tairbertaid duit ben co maccaib & daltaib,

ní bad rannaire duit fer ilmíanach,

ní bad muilleóir duit fer ilfuirig,

ní bad techtaire duit fer lonn dothengthach,

ní bad foss duit fer lesc geránach,

ní bad rúinid duit fer labar,

ní bad dáilem duit fer somesc,

ní bad dercaid duit fer drochruisc,

ní bad doraid duit fer serb sotal,

ní bad brethem duit fer condarcell,

ní bad túisech duit fer cen eólus,

ní bad cenn athchomairc duit fer dotcadach.

# Counsel The Twenty-Fifth
# From Paragraph 34
# The Counsels Of Cormac

'O son, if you listen to me,' said Cormac,
this is my counsel to you: '

Do not let a man who owes favors be your steward,

Do not let a woman with sons and foster-sons be your housekeeper,

Do not let a covetous man manage your household,

Do not let a man of much delay be your miller,

Do not let a violent foul-mouthed man your messenger,

Do not let a grumbling sluggard be your servant,

Do not let a garrulous man be your confidant,

Do not let a heavy-drinking man be your cup-bearer,

Do not let a man with a bad eyes be your watchman,

Do not let a bitter, haughty man be your doorkeeper,

Do not let an indulgent man be your judge,

Do not let a man without knowledge your leader,

Do not let an unfortunate man be your advisor.

**Abhcóide a Fiche Sé**
**Alt a Tríocha Cúig**
**Tecosca Cormaic**

'A húi Chuind, cid buidre lat rochúala?'
'Ní hansa.'

Trú cusa mberar robad,

nech ara condegar ní nád cara,

risi mná báithe.

### Counsel The Twenty-Sixth
### From Paragraph 35
### The Counsels Of Cormac

"Oh Cormac, grandson of Conn," said Cairbre,
"Who do you consider deaf in the world?"
"Easy enough,

A doomed man being given a warning,

Someone being asked an unpleasant thing,

A gossip who is told to cease prattle."

## Abhcóide a Fiche Seacht
## Alt a Fiche
## Tecosca Cormaic

'A húi Chuind, a Chormaic,' ol Carpre,
'cid as búaine for bith?'
'Ní hansa.

Fér,
umae,
ibar.'

### Counsel The Twenty-Seventh
### From Paragraph 20
### The Counsels Of Cormac

"Oh Cormac, grandson of Conn," said Cairbre,
"What is lasting in the world?"
"Easily told," said Cormac.

"Grass,
bronze,
a yew tree.
That is all."

The stark beauty of this final triad finds resonance in the Haiku of Japan. The words may be few, but the roots of meaning run deep.

The oldest surviving wooden objects in Europe, the Schöningen Spears and the La Draga bow, are both made from the wood of the yew tree. Yew's greatest claim to fame is that of its mechanical properties: despite its strength and density, Yew has an incredibly low and disproportionate modulus of elasticity at only 1,320,000 lbf/in2 (9,100 MPa). This means that the wood is extremely flexible, yet strong, making it ideally suited for use in archery bows. In fact, Yew was the wood of choice for English longbows in medieval warfare. With its straight grains, the taxin content that makes it poisonous to all wood-chewing insects, and the antimicrobial chemicals called extractives that reside in the wood long after it is cut from the tree, yew can last for millenia. The living tree can also continue to grow for thousands of years. In addition to taxin, the alkaloid ephedrine, as well as a volatile oil and traces of a cyanogenic glycoside, taxiphyllin, are also present. This means that the tree is rarely grazed by anything but deer. In addition, the tree has a number of adaptations for long life:

-Once it has reached a certain size, a yew tree can put out new shoots from the base of the trunk. As these develop they coalesce with the main trunk, appearing as buttresses around the central trunk.

-When the original trunk decays this secondary growth forms the new tree.

-While the center of a yew is rotting, a branch may put down a root into the decaying material, using the nutrients to grow anew.

-When a branch reaches the ground it can become embedded in the soil. From this point a new tree can develop, either remaining joined to the parent tree or living separately.

-A root close to the ground may also give rise to new growth at some distance from the parent tree.

-Many yews hollow out over the years. Becoming hollow can be advantageous in giving the tree greater flexibility, especially in windy conditions.

-Yews can fall and remain alive. As long as the smallest amount of root material remains connecting soil and tree, it can survive.

-Only one fungus is regularly found on the yew, the yellow polyporus sulphureus. While hastening the hollowing of the tree's center, it does not appear to harm the tree.

-Because of its great ability to produce new shoots almost anywhere on its trunk and branches, it is able to quickly heal after damage.

In Cormac's day, these truths were very well known. The tree was seen as the one creature who lived eternally.

Bronze had similar symbology and use in Cormac's world. By adding about a twelve percent measure of tin to their copper, the peoples of Northern Ireland discovered that they not only lowered the melting point of the alloy—saving valuable fuel and making the material more workable—they also created a metal that did not corrode, would not react so badly to water, and was much harder than copper alone. This was bronze. And it does indeed last many centuries, in some cases millenia. The dagger found with Racton Man, for example, was four thousand years old. Given the average lifespan of even modern people is usually under a hundred years, that is close enough to forever as makes no difference.

And grass? It is a poetic turn of phrase. But consider this: given that a grassy plain, however many battles are fought across it, will soon enough be a green and grassy plain again, I think we can see the sense of this comment. Imagine the sound of the wind over a long plain of grass on a summer day. That is, indeed, the sound of everlasting Time. World without end.

On that endless plain of grass, with the ageless wind in our ears,
our journeys with Cormac Mac Airt come to an end.

# Bibliography

Kuno Meyer, The instructions of King Cormac Mac Airt: Tecosca Cormaic in Todd lecture series (Royal Irish Academy). Volume 15, Dublin, Hodges Figgis & Co 1909

Thomas Cleary, The Counsels of Cormac: An Ancient Irish Guide to Leadership, Doubleday 2004

Joyce, Patrick Weston. A Concise History of Ireland: From the Earliest Times to 1837. Longmans, Green, and Company, 1908

Ginnell, Laurence. The Brehon laws: A legal handbook. London: TF Unwin, 1894

Wayne LaFave, Substantive Criminal Law § 13.1(e) 2d ed. 2003

McLeod, Neil. "Assault and Attempted Murder in Brehon Law." Irish Jurist (1966-) 33 (1998): 351-391.

Nagy, Joseph Falaky. "Orality in medieval Irish narrative: An overview." 1986

Thurneysen, Rudolf. "Mittelirische Verslehren." Irische Texte 3.1, 1891

David Greene. Early Irish Literature In Early Irish Society. Ed. by Myles Dillon. Dublin: Cohn O Lochlainn. 1954

Eric P. Hamp. "The Semantics of Poetry in Early Celtic." In Papers from the Thirteenth Regional Meeting of the Chicago Linguistic Society. Ed. by Woodford A. Beach, Samuel E. Fox, and Shulamith Philosoph. Chicago: Chicago Linguistic Society. 1977

Aitchison, N.B., 'Kingship, Society, and Sacrality: Rank, Power, and Ideology in Early Medieval Ireland', Traditio 49 (1994) 45-75

Binchy, D.A. (ed.), Críth Gablach, Medieval and Modern Irish Series 11. Dublin 1970

Crowe, John O'Beirne (ed. and tr.), 'Siabur-charpat Con Culaind', The Journal of the Royal Historical and Archaeological Association of Ireland 4 (1878) 371–448

Dillon, Myles, The cycles of the kings. London 1946

Jaski, Bart, Early Irish Kingship and Succession. Dublin 2000

Hull, Vernam (ed. and tr.), 'The Exile of Conall Corc', Publications of the Modern Language Association of America 56/4 (1941) 937-950

Berg, M. Early Irish Hostages: Gíall and brága in the Annals and narrative literature. MS thesis. 2016.

Smith, Colin, and James Gallen. "Cáin Adomnáin and the Laws of War." Journal of the History of International Law/Revue d'histoire du droit international 16.1 (2014): 63-81

Gilbert Markus, Adomnán's 'Law of the Innocents' Cáin Adomnáin; a Seventh Century Law for the Protection of Non-Combatants (Blackfriars Books 1997), 6.4

Dáibhí Ó Cróinín, Early Medieval Ireland, AD 400–AD 1200, (n2) 41–60

O'Brien, Browne. "Empire Vs. Tribe: The Roman Empire and the Celts". https://www.historynet.com/empire-vs-tribe-the-roman-empire-and-the-celts.htm

Binchy, Daniel A. "Bretha Crólige." Ériu (1938): 1-77.

Armbruster, G., et al. "Changes in cooking losses and sensory attributes of Angus and Holstein beef with increasing carcass weight, marbling score or longissimus ether extract." Journal of Food Science 48.3 (1983): 835-840.

Goodman, Ruth. How to be a Victorian: A Dawn-to-dusk Guide to Victorian Life. WW Norton & Company, 2014.

Kovatch, Kristen. "Crotch Mumps and Other Saddle Sores." Horse Nation: Horsing Around The World. October 13, 2015. https://www.horsenation.com/2015/10/13/crotch-mumps-and-other-saddle-sores/
Funk, William. "When Smoke Gets in Your Eyes: Regulatory Negotiation and the Public Interest-EPA's Woodstove Standards." Envtl. L. 18 (1987): 55. https://www.epa.gov/burnwise/wood-smoke-and-your-health

Stokes, Whitley. "Three Irish medical glossaries." Archiv für celtische Lexikographie 1 (1900): 325-47.

Centers for Disease Control and Prevention. "Loneliness and social isolation linked to serious health conditions." Alzheimer's Disease and Healthy Aging. https://www. cdc. gov/aging/publications/features/lonely-older-adults. html (2020).

Aldobrandino of Siena, "Li livres dou santé", British Library manuscript Sloane 2435, f. 44v.

Ginnell, Laurence. The Brehon laws: A legal handbook. London: TF Unwin, 1894.

O'Sullivan, Tomás. "Texts and Transmissions of the Scúap Chrábaid: An Old-Irish Litany in its Manuscript Context." Studia Celtica Fennica 7 (2010): 26-47.

Bergin, Osborn. Contributions to the history of palatalization in Old Irish. na, 1906.

Fomin, Maxim. "A Newly Discovered Fragment of the Early Irish Wisdom-Text Tecosca Cormaic in TCD MS 1298 (H. 2. 7)." Dimensions and Categories of Celticity: Studies in Literature and Culture. Proceedings of the Fourth International Colloquium of Societas Celto-Slavica held at the University of Łódź, Poland, 13-15 September 2009. Part 2. Studia Celto-Slavica.. Vol. 5. Lodz University Press, 2010.

Ford, Patrick K. "Pagan past and Christian present: Some aspects of the problem." Études celtiques 29.1 (1992): 457-458.

Fomin, Maxim. "Tecosca Cormaic: the compilation of a wisdom-text" University of Ulster at Coleraine, 21 November 2003. 9-16.

Daniewski, Wlodzimierz M., et al. "Why the yew tree (Taxus baccata) is not attacked by insects." Phytochemistry 49.5 (1998): 1279-1282.

Schwarcz, Joe. "The Right Chemistry: The yew tree has been a valuable weapon." The Montreal Gazette, December 16, 2016

Antolín, Ferran, et al. "An integrated perspective on farming in the early Neolithic lakeshore site of La Draga (Banyoles, Spain)." Environmental Archaeology 19.3 (2014): 241-255.

Schoch, Werner H., et al. "New insights on the wooden weapons from the Paleolithic site of Schöningen." Journal of human evolution 89 (2015): 214-225.

Partridge, Tim. "Trees in Mythology, Legend, Symbolism and Religion." Ancient Yew Group 3 (1993).

Bevan-Jones, Robert. The ancient yew: a history of Taxus baccata. Windgather Press, 2016.

Manning, W. H. "Ironworking in the Celtic world." The Celtic World (1995): 310-320.

Needham, Stuart, et al. "Death by combat at the dawn of the Bronze Age? Profiling the dagger-accompanied burial from Racton, West Sussex." The Antiquaries Journal 97 (2017): 65-117.

Savage, George, A Concise History of Bronzes, Frederick A. Praeger, Inc. Publishers, New York, 1968 p. 17

## About the Author

Olivia Wylie is a professional landscaper who specializes
in the restoration of neglected gardens. In days of rain or snow she creates works
revolving around the connections between human and green lives.
She lives in Denver with a very patient husband
and a rather impatient cat.

www.ingramcontent.com/pod-product-compliance
Lightning Source LLC
Chambersburg PA
CBHW061111070526
44583CB00027B/3261